Excellent, excellent, excellent! This story of an atypical American family in a typical American town stands out for its unique perspective and its ability to bring larger issues into sharp focus. The authors' thoughts, feelings, and experiences reach through the pages to tug at our heartstrings. I literally could not put it down.

> — Skip Norman, Hewlett-Packard engineering education liaison to minority-serving colleges and universities (retired) and recipient, Congressional Black Caucus Education Technology Leadership Award

American Family is terrific — I read it in one sitting.

> — Bob Saldich, CEO, Raychem (retired), and former chair, The Commonwealth Club

It is heartbreaking and shocking that this entire saga could possibly be happening in our own most progressive and affluent communities. And, it inspires hope for the human spirit that there are two good and brave souls out there who can help lead the way into a kinder world.

> — Esther Hewlett, co-founder, New Global Citizens and former board member, Global Fund for Women

This book is affecting on so many levels — as a story about gay, lesbian, bisexual and transsexual people who refuse to be defined by what they're not, as a story of adoptive parents and all that entails, and as a story about "things racial," in the authors' words. It made me cry — because I was moved and because I can relate.

> — Ed Gurowitz, Ph.D., consultant and writer

This book is a testimony to what love and family are really about. Two remarkable women set out to share their love with children of a different race and social circumstances. Perhaps naïvely, they acted on their commitment to justice and equality. To their eternal credit, they stayed the course through the kind of situations that might use up most people's reservoir of courage. Over and over, they faced the brutality of America's unspoken reality: Blatant racism lives on despite the social gains of the last 50 years. Anyone in need of a good dose of valor should read this book. This is the kind of heroism that doesn't make the evening news. What it does make is an enormous difference in the life of a remarkable American family. This is a love story, but unlike a romance novel, this one makes the reader angry. It also fosters the hope that love can triumph even in the most trying of circumstances.

— *Rev. Dr. Mari Castellanos,*
United Church of Christ clergy

I was touched, angered, softened and opened by reading the story of this courageous American family. I saw my own prejudices more clearly and found myself more able to own my part in stereotyping others who I imagine are not like me. If Barb, Stacy and their kids can find compassion in their hearts to keep trying in the face of how "our America" continues to operate, then it is a clarion call to all of us to discover a future that is worthy of our best efforts — one that we can all feel proud to be a part of. As this honest and heartfelt story attests, we have a long way to go. We can do no less than stand up for the American values we believe in that have yet to be fulfilled. The future of millions of our children and grandchildren hangs in the balance.

— *Juanita Brown, Ph.D., co-founder,* The World Café *and author,* The World Café: Shaping Our Futures through Conversations that Matter

I thank Barb Waugh and Stacy Cusulos for their inspiration, for keeping on keeping on. Their energy is contagious, light and uplifting, evidence of an unquenchable Spirit.

— *Lewis Brown Griggs, speaker, trainer and coach*

Barbara Waugh and Stacy Cusulos, two white middle-class professionals, adopted two black children and raised them in a prosperous suburb near a highly diverse city. This choice became a story of love and grief, stretching across a divide that is typically ignored in the U.S. — between black and white people, rich and poor schools, adored and defamed children, peaceful and violent communities. This book is a quiet, lingering, compelling wake-up call for people on all sides of the divide.

— *Art Kleiner, editor-in-chief,* strategy+business *magazine and author,* The Age of Heretics

Empathy is our most critical human characteristic, a key to our survival as a species. Stacy Cusulos and Barbara Waugh have produced an engrossing story that is an effective vehicle for exploring who we are and what we need to change if the world's families are going to live and thrive as one. *American Family* is an important book that every American should read.

— *Mark Albion, Ph.D., New York Times best-selling author, co-founder, Net Impact and More Than Money Careers*

I love how specific Stacy Cusulos and Barb Waugh are in conveying what is helpful and what is not. They both are so real in their communication — and we *have* to have honest conversations if we are going to make any significant progress.

—*Barb Harris, former editor-in-chief,* Shape *magazine*

American Family: Things Racial is one the most poignant, grace filled, and loving tributes added to the landscape of books addressing race matters in North America. It chronicles the attempt to make sense of a family's destabilized home life, which is turned upside down and inside out because of skin color. This book will subtly transform your heart, elevate your soul and expand your mind. It is a must read no matter what your preconceived notions about race or family. Page after riveting page, this is the quintessential story of the American family.

— Rev. Dr. Bentley de Bardelaben, executive for administration and communication, United Church of Christ

Like a musical fugue, the recurring theme is really about the triumph of love — of Barb and Stacy for each other, and together for their kids; of the neighbor whose caring surmounted her racism and homophobia so that she lovingly prepared dinner for the tired family at the end of the day; of the parents and grandparents whose love transcended centuries of religious tradition and deeply held cultural beliefs to fully embrace Stacy, Barb and their kids; and of the love encountered in unexpected places. Love really wins!

— Eugenie Prime, M.A., M.S., M.B.A., former manager, Global Libraries and Information Centers, Hewlett-Packard, and former chair, Board of Regents of the National Library of Medicine

This book is one powerful statement. About many things. At first I couldn't embrace how these two women made the choice to parent these two Black kids. Before the end of the book, I was feeling, How could they not?

— Mark Alter, M.S.W., therapist

Barb Waugh and Stacy Cusulos are more than parents, they are trailblazers. They have uncovered and looked straight in the eye of some terrible problems that impact our children, including the failures of our schools, police services, welfare services, and other systems of "care." With this book they confront the disheartening lack of awareness and understanding that most people have about these problems. They are problem solvers advancing solutions for all children.

— Carol Lamont, antipoverty advocate and award-winning foundation professional

An eye-opener beyond compare, *American Family* is a work of courage and love. Everyone not belonging to a targeted minority group should read this book. It is truly astounding to learn the degree to which other people's negative expectations can cause utter havoc in an innocent life.

— Rudite Emir, author, lecturer, project manager, mother and grandmother

Barbara Waugh and Stacy Cusulos recognize that the cookie-cutter parenting promoted by glossy magazines will leave most children behind. Critical social analysis — macro and micro — is necessary to make sense of the systems that oppress and to construct healthy and just alternatives. While their family has paid a high price for this knowledge, hopefully this book about it will save others a good deal.

— Mary E. Hunt, Ph.D., Women's Alliance for Theology, Ethics and Ritual

This courageous and authentic book tells the story of an ever-evolving tapestry of love woven through deep relationships. It is an example for all of us who struggle with our stereotypes and unconscious racist behaviors. It opened my eyes and renewed my determination to live more racially free.

— *Monique Sternin, co-founder and senior advisor,*
Positive Deviance Initiative, Tufts University

I could not put down *American Family* once I started to read it, staying up until 3 a.m. the first night. The heartbreaking revelations and soul-searching quest for truth gripped my soul. The emotional richness of this book provides a deeply moving portrayal of life in America. All of our children have important gifts and talents to contribute to our community. *American Family* clearly depicts the needs of children of color, their trials and tribulations at school and in our larger society. The question that *American Family* evoked in me is this: How can we create educational experiences where our children are seen at a deep level and bond with their true selves, and where they can have an authentic connection with others?

—*Diego James Navarro, founder, director and instructor,*
Academy for College Excellence

Stacy Cusulos and Barb Waugh's journey has brought them both great insight. And what resilience they have demonstrated! I'm sure their story will raise a lot of questions for a lot of people and that's the conversation we need more of in this country.

— *Bob Sadler, CEO, Sadler Consulting*

With candor, honesty and tenderness, this story unfolds with all of its struggles and joys so that we are drawn into it as witnesses of the power of love. In this case — two white lesbians raising two adopted African-American children — it takes "more than a village" to raise young ones. It takes a full comprehension of the dynamics of oppression and a large dose of self-awareness. This story is being lived out all across our country and for those of us who are witnesses, our task is to create communities of caring and justice with real appreciation of that intricate web of life that holds us all.

— *Loey Powell, national staff, United Church of Christ*

I am truly grateful for this story, though at times just reading it was almost too much. I can't imagine what it was like to live it. It seems like racism is woven into our cellular structure and we need to eliminate it one strand at a time. Or perhaps it is like Nobel prizewinner Ilya Prigogine said when he was asked how scientific revolutions occur: The old scientists have to die and new ones take their place. My deepest wish is that our children's children benefit from the fight these two women continue to fight.

— *Pele Rouge Chadima, co-founder,*
Resonance: Timeless Earth Wisdom

American Family is a unique, courageous and starkly revealed history of individuals and a culture on so many levels. It is also a powerful reminder of the everyday necessity to keep exposing and healing the effects of racism.

— *Beclee Wilson, poet and teacher*

Barb Waugh and Stacy Cusulos have written an important and very readable book. Their story of raising two African-American children in an upscale northern California suburb is by turns inspiring, shocking and heartbreaking, as they suffer from the hatreds of others and bravely confront a few prejudices of their own. Racism, they remind us, is alive and well in the age of Obama; the American promise of equal rights and dignity for all has yet to be realized.

— *Marc Gunther, contributing editor, FORTUNE; senior writer, GreenBiz.com; blogger, The Energy Collective*

This chronicle of two well-intentioned, highly intelligent and devoted white women's experiences in the adoption and rearing of two African-American children in current day America is a searing indictment of the racism and homophobia still rampant in our country. Far more than a cautionary tale, the unadorned anecdotal style makes the reader wince with the pain and injustice inflicted on these children, but it also reveals great depths of compassion, courage and immense love, often from unexpected sources. In spite of their frustration and hurt, these talented writers offer a positive message of hope, and their story just may inspire you to behave a lot differently in the future.

— *Joel Birnbaum, senior vice president of R&D, Hewlett-Packard (retired)*

I laughed and wept and sighed and yearned my way through the story of Barb, Stacy, Shawna, Stephen and Jamal. If the authors' goal was to change people, they can count me among their indicators of success.

— *The Reverend Greg Ward, senior minister, Unitarian Church of the Monterey Peninsula*

American Family: Things Racial is a handbook for confronting life's injustices. It's about the unrelenting opportunities we have to take heroic measures every day rather than "live inside" and ignore them. That's who Barb and Stacy are — two she-roes, as Maya Angelou would put it — who tirelessly confronted authorities, institutions and people for the overt and covert acts of racism that their children were subjected to on a regular basis.

— Shelly Gordon-Gray, public relations business owner, journalist, mediator

I was riveted by the story of this family. It rang some painfully familiar bells — I have lived in a community like theirs for more than 30 years and suffered from its judgmental nature. Even though my children and I are white, as a single parent family we stood out. These judgments about anyone "different" hurt everyone. This story also made me examine my own perceptions.

— Kirby Giaramita, artist and small business owner

In their new book, *American Family,* Barbara Waugh and Stacy Cusulos are inviting us into a most intimate journey of hope, devastation, racism and resilience as they navigate through the twists and turns of life. I was moved to tears as I read each heart-wrenching detail and found myself asking myself over and over: "How can this be happening in my country? What can I, as one person, start doing or stop doing to eliminate racism?" You won't be the same person after reading this book — and that is a good thing!

— Rayona Sharpnack, founder and CEO, Institute for Women's Leadership

Often, when we read about issues related to racism and homophobia, statistics are cited. Yes, statistics are important; however, they represent real people with the tears washed away. Stacy Cusulos and Barbara Waugh have written a riveting book that invites people to open not only their minds but their hearts. Through the intimate and powerful sharing of their life together and the lives of their two African-American children, we journey with them as they love, nurture and celebrate family while fighting blatant racism and homophobia.

— Ann Hanson, minister for sexuality education
and justice, United Church of Christ

American Family: Things Racial is an interracial family story borne out of the idealism of two courageous modern white lesbian feminists shaped by the politics of the 1960s. Cusulos and Waugh fought to keep their adopted Black son and daughter safe from the horrors of racial profiling, raw discrimination and other deeply embedded prejudices and stereotypes endemic in American society. With its directness and honesty, this book is authentic. Through their story we learn that "things racial" are in us, both as burden and blessing. Moreover, if we accept the challenge that comes with understanding and struggle, we will one day become the change we want to see.

— Brenda Joyner, professor of sociology,
Lorain County Community College

I used to live in the town where this book takes place. Had you asked me, I would have said that the community was idyllic: a bastion of well-educated and socially progressive people. The one huge difference, though, is that I was afforded the white privilege that obviously eluded Barb and Stacy's children. It pains me to read of the shabby treatment given to two women who deserve nothing less than to be lauded as heroines.

— *Jay Davidson, teacher, speaker, writer and author of* Teach Your Children Well: A Teacher's Advice for Parents

Barbara Waugh and Stacy Cusulos made extraordinary sacrifices for the children they love. I know the challenges that confront new parents who suddenly find themselves with a young baby and no owner's manual. Barb and Stacy's experiences and the particular challenges they faced as two moms crossing the racial divide — and meeting every new day with courage and creativity — are awe-inspiring.

— *Ray Offenheiser, president, Oxfam America*

American Family is an honest and courageous book about two persistent and destructive realities of our society: homophobia and racism. It is the story of how two brave women cared for their two African-American children — in the face of depressingly constant societal pressures — with strength, love and kindness. Read it to be informed and inspired.

— *Anne Firth Murray, founding president,* *Global Fund for Women, and* *consulting professor, Stanford University*

I always wanted to write a play that would begin with someone arguing with God before the world is created that just making people's skin different colors wouldn't pose great enough challenges for human beings and their spiritual growth. Then we would cut to scenes, say, from these children's lives, or anywhere else on the planet, to show how wrong they were. Here is a book to show that meeting these challenges fully could bring us to the level of saints and bodhisattvas, or at least to the level of being fully human.

— *Rhoberta Hirtir, co-founder, Deep Nurturing*

Having experienced a workshop based on the first printing of this book, I can say it was a very engaging and non-threatening way to begin meaningful conversation about racial issues and the impact of racism. Stacy Cusulos and her colleague, Diane Woods, are experienced facilitators who are easily accessible to participants, balance their energies well, and model effective teamwork.

— *Ann Todd Jealous, consultant, cultural diversity trainer, writer*

American Family

Things Racial

Stacy Cusulos, M.Div.
and Barbara Waugh, Ph.D.

Authors' Note

All names but our own have been changed, and most events have had their identifying details changed.

Our story is not about the town we lived in or the people we have come up against or been helped by, except as a microcosm of the struggle and victories for family in America — on a national as well as local scale. An adjacent white town is worse, from all reports of friends there. Another adjacent town, more racially mixed and much easier about race, is worse in a different way. In that town things are worked out more often with guns and knives than with words or silence, denial, sabotage or indifference.

No matter the town, the people, the details of names or a specific experience, the American family has come a long way since the founding of this country, has come a long way in our own lifetimes. And no matter the town, the American family still has a way to go to make justice a reality for all of God's children.

Now is the time to make justice a reality for all of God's children.

— Dr. Martin Luther King, Jr.
"I Have a Dream," August 28, 1963

Though this nation has proudly thought of itself as an ethnic melting pot, in things racial we have always been and continue to be … a nation of cowards … Though there remain many unresolved racial issues in this nation, we, average Americans, simply do not talk enough with each other about race.

— Attorney General Eric Holder
February 18, 2009

TABLE OF CONTENTS

FOREWORD

By Adam Kahane, author of
Power and Love: A Theory and Practice of Social Change

Oppression is harder to see from above than from below. While people on top experience themselves as simply and innocently getting on with living their lives, those underneath experience themselves as cruelly held back. When such crucial aspects of the way our society works are invisible to us, we can only flail around, confused and angry. If we want to change how things work, we need to be able to see and grasp these unjust and asymmetrical dynamics.

American Family: Things Racial offers us three great gifts. The first is that it starkly illuminates the dynamics of power. Stacy Cusulos and Barbara Waugh have experienced power from both above and below, and their unusual binocular perspective helps us all see more. Furthermore, they tell their stories straightforwardly and personally, with both clear minds and broken-open hearts. Their book therefore leaves us unable to avert our gaze and to claim that we do not see.

Stacy and Barbara help us see that we are not — as individuals, communities and societies — as innocent or superior as we often imagine ourselves to be. They show us ways in which they, their town and the U.S. are, in essence, as unfair and violent as those in any other war zone. This realization can humble us and open us up to changing what we are doing and the terrible results we are creating.

1

A second gift that Stacy and Barbara give us is a pointer to what we need to do if we want to change this reality. All of us have a "power" drive to realize ourselves. Our power morphs from generative "power to" to degenerative "power over" when we turn away from or deny the humanity and "power to" of others. This is the dehumanizing and oppressive "othering" that the authors have witnessed.

But they have also witnessed how, conversely, our power can morph from degenerative to generative when we can reconnect with the humanity of others. All of us also have this "love" drive to unite the separated. Love is not only the empathetic recognition of the humanity of others, but the felt sense of the interconnectedness and oneness of us all. The authors show us that love operates not only in reconnecting with our family and allies, but also, crucially, in reconnecting with our opponents: those who have othered us and whom we have othered.

If we want to change the reality of our world, we therefore need love. But love is not all we need. Martin Luther King, Jr., said, "Power without love is reckless and abusive, and love without power is sentimental and anemic." Stacy and Barbara's third gift is to demonstrate, through the stories of their struggles, how we need to work on employing both our love and our power. They reach out, embrace, confront, retreat, attack and fight on. If we want to create a better world, so must we all.

PREFACE

Our son is 5 years old and in kindergarten. It's bedtime and I am in his room to tuck him in and kiss him goodnight. He has had a rough day at school and as he turns his head toward me, I see tears streaming down his face.

I ask him why he's crying.

"I want to die, Mommy. I don't want to be brown anymore."

I feel like someone has just stabbed me in the heart.

*   *   *

We are white. Our two children, adopted at birth, are Black. We raised them with the loving help of our friends and our community, both Black and white. As for most parents, raising our kids has been the most rewarding journey of our lives. It has also been utterly heartbreaking.

Time and again, we found that in spite of our white privilege, money, advanced education, professional positions, plus our long experience in fighting — and beating — the system, and the famously liberal area in which we live, we could not protect our children from devastating racism.

Starting from the day Shawna and Stephen left the warm cocoon of our family home for preschool, our daughter and son consistently ran into a degree of ignorance and cruelty (both subtle and blatant) that we didn't want to admit existed in our country, let alone in the progressive college town in which we live. We thought our

3

children would be safe here. We thought they'd be safe with us as their parents.

They weren't. Facing this ugly truth again and again was a chronic and recurring wakeup call. Were we failing as parents? Was there really nothing we could do to protect our children from the narrow-mindedness and hatred of others?

Luckily, we had a second wakeup call, one that opened the way to resolving some of the situations our kids were thrust into. We came to realize that we would never make an ounce of progress with all the teachers, parents, and police officers whose behavior was hurting our children until we admitted that we were just as human — and flawed — as they were. We had to acknowledge that we, too, had unconscious beliefs about who was better, who was right, who was more ethical or more spiritual or more sincere. We, too, had hurt people with our beliefs. We, too, were contributing to the prevailing "us vs. them" mentality. We "knew," for example, that the entire Greek side of our extended family hated Blacks and gays, that a white principal would never stand up for our son against a band of white parents, and that the cops would never be on our side. (Fortunately, we were wrong. Many times.)

As it turned out, whenever we dehumanized other people by labeling them "racists" or "homophobes" and ignoring who they were as individuals, we were demolishing any possibility of improving the situation for our kids. We came to see that admitting our own biases and sharing this uncomfortable, all-too-human common ground was the only workable starting point for talking with people about racism (or any other "ism"). And talking about it was only the starting point for improving things.

Whenever we succeeded in changing the way some people looked at and treated our children, it was because we approached them in a spirit of shared humanity and they were willing to change. This is not to say that we didn't lose it at times. We did, many times. But as time went on, we got better at not being self-righteously right. We changed, too. "They" changed us — and for the better. We learned how to stand in a place of common humanity long enough to move things forward with people we once called our enemies.

Life has dealt all of us far more pain than we ever expected. But as parents and now grandparents, we've also experienced far more love and joy than we ever imagined possible in our lives. Most days we're not bitter, or angry or in despair. We're in this for the long haul, good and bad, feeling the pain of the racial wound in America and working to help heal it. We've learned there is no "us" and "them." It's all us. Together we've come a long way in America, and together, we can complete the course.

WELCOME TO OUR WORLD

STACY

Our microcosm, like any other, reflects the larger whole. There is a connection between the sense of isolation and hopelessness we often experienced because of who we are — white lesbian moms raising adopted Black children — and the larger sense of isolation, hopelessness, and despair that is at the root of the violence and destruction here in the U.S. and around the globe. There is a connection between the victory over isolation and hopelessness we sometimes felt, and the larger sense that the world can work for everyone manifested so wonderfully and often, here in the U.S. and worldwide.

There is also a connection between what we have learned and the positive actions we and those around us are taking as an extended family and the direction we could take as a larger human family. We share our story in order to contribute to our world. We share as openly as possible in the hope that what we have to say can be useful. We offer our ideas on how to move from fear and confusion about what is different to knowing and embracing those differences as aspects of the wider self. We believe separation is an illusion, a flimsy barrier to what unites us: knowing and experiencing our profound connection to one another.

BARB

When I was in college in the 60s, I was active in the early Civil Rights Movement, participated in the

Freedom Schools[1], the walk-outs, and a cross-dating project between the white and Black state colleges, which commenced with the warning by our campus minister, "Watch out for white men driving slowly — they may have guns...." I once even stood with my back to Angela Davis, protecting her with my body as a security guard, scanning the audience for people who might try to shoot her. I was also involved in many long discussions about race and racism during the women's movement. So I was not completely clueless about race in America. But until I became the mother of two Black children and was myself adopted and tutored by African-American friends, I didn't realize just how clueless "not completely clueless" really was.

We are sharing here what we've learned about race and racism beyond the obvious level of cross burning, n-word graffiti, and the patterns of arrests and imprisonments in our country. We hope our story will be useful to those who read it, and help contribute to the progress America as a country is making at healing the racial divide in America, beginning with describing the invisible ways we can hurt and help each other with race never being mentioned. I grew up in the South, with "colored" and "white" drinking fountains, sections of the bus and movie theaters, strictly segregated schools, and no such thing as lesbians or gay men. In my lifetime,

---

[1] These were free alternative schools for African-American children to attend when they boycotted regular school, thus causing the state to lose federal matching funds. They were a strategy in the early Civil Rights movement.

miracles that I could never have imagined have occurred, moving the American family into an institution for all God's children.

Ours is not a story of triumph or resolution. In many ways it's flawed, not least by our own prejudices and limited thinking, and by being only our side of the stories that always involved others, whose stories we cannot tell because the dialogue never got that far. We expect dialogue in this country to continue and deepen, and we rejoice in that possibility. We offer up the story of our hopes, dreams, heartaches and despair, triumphs and achievements in the hope that it contributes to the ongoing blessed and miraculous creation of American family for all God's children.

PART I:
ADOPTION
TO ELEMENTARY SCHOOL

Walking Through the Veil

BARB

I don't know what it is to grow up Black in this country, but I know what it is to love someone who is — and it's the most joy and the most pain I have ever known.

Meeting my children's birth mothers, coming to love them and share the pain of their broken dreams and relentlessly cruel worlds, I walk through the invisible veil that until then has separated me from the devastating reality of poverty and racism in America. Soon, thanks to the injustices my two Black children are confronted with, even as toddlers, I become a full-time resident on the other side of that veil, someone who is fighting, for their sake, to remove the veil that separates Black and white, rich and poor, gay and straight.

'It's Not About You'

STACY

Our journey together has taught us that there is more than racism and poverty keeping people on the sunless side of the veil that separates the people in charge from the people struggling to get out from under. All the other "-isms" and "-phobias" play a part too. It's a place I know well, a place I was consigned to even before Barb and I become the parents of two Black babies.

In 1978, fresh out of divinity school, I am offered a wonderful job, as Youth and Young Adult Minister for over a hundred northern California churches in the denomination into which I will soon be ordained. Before that can happen, though, a woman minister in the region calls my boss to ask if he's lost his mind, hiring a lesbian to head up youth programs for our churches. The whole thing escalates, and although my ordination goes through as planned, I am soon on trial before a church tribunal for alleged "theological incompetence."

At my trial, my boss, a Japanese-American from Hawaii, speaks his truth — and puts his job on the line. "I do not understand homosexuality," he testifies. "I am not sure how to interpret the Bible about it, either. What I am sure of is this: What is happening to Stacy feels exactly like what happened to me in my own first job after ordination, right after World War II. Churches rose up against my boss for hiring 'a dirty Jap.' This is all I know about the matter, and it dictates the course of action I propose to follow."

Thanks to his passionate defense, I am "cleared of all charges" of alleged theological incompetence related to my sexuality, and am able to retain my job as the youth minister. Many churches, however, refuse to let me in their doors. They don't want me contaminating their youth. Among some of the wealthiest churches, talk continues for months of withdrawing their money and membership in the denomination. I cannot count the number of church members who come up to me, touch my hand, and assure me, "This isn't about you, it's about the issue."

Of course their stance is about me. I *am* the issue. That's what hurts. In my experience, people who start out with "It's not you, it's the issue..." are about to do something very hurtful to real people, hurtful actions they are attempting to take no responsibility for. At least be responsible!

Preparing the Ground

BARB

Nine years into our relationship, Stacy and I decide to take the plunge. We are going to adopt a baby — at least we hope we are. We both have good jobs in Silicon Valley's computer industry. Stacy has long since left the church, heartbroken at the subtle and overt bigotry she encountered there. We are in a big rambling house in the Bay Area in preparation for starting a family.

We have talked off and on for years about having kids and have finally decided that we do want children, but we would rather help a child who has no home than give birth to one of our own. I am thrilled with our decision. It has always been a dream of mine to be a mother. Now it's going to happen!

Entering the Adoption Maze
STACY

We come from a place of status and privilege. We are white, well educated, financially stable, and proactive in dealing with bureaucracies. But despite all these advantages, our first attempt at adoption — through our county agency — reminds us, in no uncertain terms, that we belong on the powerless side of the veil.

First we have to accept the fact that Barb must do the adoption as a single parent. Because we are two women, we can't get married, despite the fact that we've lived together now for 10 years. And if we're not married, we can't adopt together. However, as a member of Barb's household, I will also be rigorously screened. The child will have Barb's last name. My last name will be our child's middle name, and we will pay thousands of dollars and undergo yet another process for me to get "legal guardianship" so we can protect our kids in the event anything should happen to Barb. (Many years later, when it becomes legally possible in California, I file for and — after yet another rigorous evaluation and thousands of dollars more — am granted co-adoption parental status.)

Finally, our screening begins. The social worker we are assigned asks Barb, "How do lesbians do it?" Barb asks for clarification, and it turns out this woman wants a description of lesbian sex! Barb suggests some books for her to read. She chides Barb (who has a Ph.D. in organizational psychology) for making more money than she does and urges Barb to find her a job in the well-regarded company she works for. Barb wonders if finding this woman a job is the only way she'll grant us a child.

My own interview includes a point-blank question about whether I am planning to molest our child and questions about why else we might be thinking of adopting if not for that reason. Our interviews conclude with a recommendation by the adoption agency that only a boy 12 years or older would be appropriate for us. The social worker explains that she figures as lesbians we wouldn't molest a boy, and if he's 12, he'll be old enough to tell authorities if we do.

On first reading this report we are numb. Then, embarrassed and ashamed. For days we can't discuss it. And then, we are enraged. This is not right. We are fine with a 12-year-old boy, but not for these reasons. We have to do something. What?

At this point we walk a razor's edge that will become very familiar over the years: taking on the system to remove roadblocks hurled onto our path by homophobia, racism, and general ignorance, but not to the extent that it derails us from our goals, in this case, to adopt a child. We call friends all over the place, and discover that one of our friends, a lesbian, has a sister who heads up the entire county agency that authorizes adoptions.

We go to the sister and present our notes from these interviews. She is chagrined and apologetic, and promises us that we will have a different social worker.

We are assigned another social worker who is much better, but who isn't very hopeful for us. She explains, "You won the battle, but you lost the war. All the social workers are now aligned against you because you escalated to the head of the agency. We're like a union and we watch out for each other. You've got a reputation at the agency now of causing trouble. They don't want you to get a child."

This reputation has catalyzed a boycott of us among those who decide on the allocation of kids, but our new social worker assures us that she can tell from our interview with her that we will be good parents, and she can get us a child. Her sister is a lesbian and a good mother. Will we take a baby with Down Syndrome? We say yes.

But after months of waiting, we give up on the county. We hire two lawyers specializing in private adoptions, and learn that our most likely chance is to adopt a "hard to place" baby. This term is applied to any child born with a disability, any child who is racially mixed, and all children who are African-American. The fact that healthy children of color are labeled — and in fact *are* — "hard to place" makes us crazy.

We talk a lot about our prospects and agree to adopt a child with a disability or a racially mixed child. As two white women, however, we feel inadequate to raising an African-American child: We have never had to learn, and therefore can't teach, the survival skills an African-American child needs to grow up in this country. We know that our commitment to and our history of activism in the Civil Rights movement has taught us a lot, but they have also revealed how little we truly understand about what it means to be Black in this country. We see the oppression of Black people as the deepest, most pernicious form of discrimination, worse than that against people of any other race or those with disabilities. We see the journey in our country to end racism as the longest journey. We believe we're not the best choice for raising a Black girl or boy: It wouldn't be fair to the child.

One day we get a call from our attorneys: They have a child for us and we must be in their office within the next three hours. We rush to the office and learn that the child is African-American. Her mother has had no prenatal care, so it is unknown if there are disabilities.

We say this is not the right baby for us because this baby is Black, and we explain our reasoning. The lawyers listen patiently, smile, and tell us that our daughter will be with us in a week or less. We again insist that we are not the right parents for this child, and then the lawyers tell us what we already know: There aren't enough Black families to take all the children who need homes; thousands of Black children spend their whole lives being shuffled back and forth between foster homes — most often white foster homes — sometimes with people who do it only for the money paid to foster parents.

Driving home from this meeting in a daze, we accept that a baby is coming and we are going to be her parents. Five days later, our newborn arrives. She has a heart-shaped face, gorgeous brown eyes, and a full, beautiful head of hair. We name her Shawna.

It's said that bonding with a child can be instantaneous. That is definitely our experience. We are goners. Shawna is curious, feisty, and insists on instant gratification. One minute to heat up her milk is one minute too long!

Nine months later the county adoption agency calls and offers us a 2-year-old Caucasian little girl. We are up to our necks with our new responsibilities and full-time jobs so we thank them profusely but decline to adopt a second child at this point.

Warm Hearts, Warm Welcome
BARB

Life with our new daughter is beautiful. We've never been happier! Crazy as it sounds, I'm also even more thrilled with my job than I had been before the adoption: specifically with the medical plan that covers her care, coverage far superior to any our baby would have gotten though the welfare system or the pathetic health plans I was on before joining my current company. My previous $6,000 annual salary with no benefits, from the women's center for a consortium of theological schools, was too shaky a foundation on which to start a family. That's why I am now in corporate drag putting my Ph.D. to work with high tech, which I have now decided is the hub of corporate America and now seems to run the country and maybe the world.

I am nervous about the reactions of my birth family to our adopting a Black child — I grew up in the South — and have not told them what Stacy and I were planning. My late grandfather once bragged to me of his Ku Klux Klan affiliation, and although my parents and most of my extended family are very liberal, I still hesitate, not wanting anything to dampen our joy over our baby girl.

I call my middle sister, Lizzie, to get her thoughts on what to do about telling our folks. She advises writing a letter so they can have their shock in private and express their first reaction without witnesses. I write the letter, expressing our joy, our hopes and dreams, and include a picture of the three of us.

My parents call. They are thrilled for us! Two days later a huge Fed-Ex'ed box of baby clothes arrives, along with a bouquet welcoming Shawna Cusulos Waugh, the newest member of the family. Later, my youngest sister, Maggie, tells me that when the letter arrived, Mom whooped for joy and called Daddy to come in from the yard. From the instant they got the news, their reaction was pure joy. Mom and Dad figure Shawna's definitely in the right family — her birthday is the same month in which Lizzie, Dad and Maggie were born.

I am stunned: Who are these people I thought I knew so well? I never imagined this wonderful reaction. I am thrilled, relieved beyond belief, and totally chagrined at my own prejudice.

A Matched Set of Baby Showers

STACY

When Shawna arrives, Barb and I are working at the same Fortune 100 company, though in different divisions miles apart. Although we haven't formally come out as a couple and anti-gay jokes still abound at the water cooler, we suspect a lot of people know. Even so we are shocked when our co-workers throw each of us a baby shower that the two divisions have coordinated, so one gets us the stroller and the other the playpen! Who are these people we privately had suspected as homophobic, and all living in Ozzie and Harriet families?

We are very touched and grateful. Not only do these parties acknowledge Barb's and my relationship, they also show love and respect for us and our daughter, and for our family as a family like any other, needing playpens, strollers, and baby showers!

We had assumed that people wouldn't "get it" and might even discriminate against us in some way. Not true. They chose to focus on the things we have in common, that unite us, rather than on the things that separate us, our differences.

Rich conversations start even before the baby showers and we get lots of help with colic, recommendations about the best baby doctors, and brand-new-seeming hand-me-downs.

Gaining an Auntie

BARB

Shawna's personality emerges very quickly. She's funny, stubborn, and energetic. Then one day when she's about 3 months old, I hold her up to the mirror to see herself. She takes one look and bursts into tears! I realize in that moment that the only faces baby Shawna has seen up close are white ones.

I grab the phone and soon I'm on the line with a woman I know only from work. Janine James is a VP at my company and normally I'd never ask her a personal favor, but Shawna's cries have knocked any concern for propriety right out of the ring. A stunningly gorgeous Black woman, Janine is six feet tall with a shaved head molded like Cleopatra's and skin the color of dark chocolate.

In tears, I start babbling about my fantasy that over the next decade we'd get to know each other better and then as my daughter headed into the teenage years I could ask Janine to teach Shawna all about Black hair and make-up, but that I couldn't wait ten years, I needed her now, because my daughter needed to be held by her, to see her face, to see herself with Janine.

To which Janine replies calmly, "What can I do to help?"

"Come over as soon as possible," I beg.

She comes over after work that very day, and it's the first of many visits, family dinners, and holidays we spend with Janine, our first official auntie, and the first member of what will grow to be our large and always loving and often quite critical African-American extended family.

Safe at Home

STACY

Our first couple of years with Shawna are a mix of great joy, very little sleep, and very hard work. Shawna is like a blooming flower — each stage perfect, but even more splendid and full a day later. It takes six months to find a breakthrough with the colic, a solution that finally allows us all to sleep for more than an hour at a time.

There is (as yet) no family leave for adoptive parents — just leave without pay. We're so worried about all the adoption and other new-baby bills that we keep working full-time — and so also have a childcare bill!

Our daughter is incredibly beautiful in every way. But we slowly begin to discover what it means for us to have an African-American child. Inside our home, we feel safe, protected, and blessed most of the time. Outside, we experience curiosity, confusion, and at times, outright hostility. Inside, we are just two people raising a child. Outside, we are often seen as "the other." One day we are in the mall with her at 3 months when an Asian family asks us very bluntly, but with total friendliness, "Why ever did you adopt a *Black* baby?" We explain that we wanted a child who needed parents, and more Black children than white children are in this situation. In the grocery store, a sister of the night toddles over in spike heels to Barb, looks at Shawna, and sniffs, "Your old man musta sure been dark!" A racially mixed social worker looks at us like we're crazy... aren't we aware of the National Association of Black Social Workers' stand that cross-racial adoption amounts to genocide? She wants to know what on earth we were thinking. We ask her what she thinks the alternatives are, and we have a tense and mutually unenlightening conversation.

Another Baby?

STACY

When Shawna is 2½, Barbara has haunting dreams that someone in our family is missing, that it isn't yet complete.

Barb is also interviewing for a promotion to a job in another state, in a small city close to both ocean and mountains. She comes back from the interview deeply saddened. It will never work for our family, she says. The area is beautiful, but very anti-gay and there are no people of color. She feels more urgently than ever that we open up to finding our missing child. Compared to moving to a conservative rural town, adopting another child feels minor to me, and I agree.

We decide we want an African-American baby sister for our daughter — this way Shawna won't be the only Black person in the family, and we already know how to raise a girl. We contact the adoption lawyers and eventually they call to say they've heard from a pregnant young Black woman who's 18 years old with a 2-year-old already. She can't keep the baby she's carrying and still finish high school.

Barbara forms a wonderful relationship with this young woman by phone — she lives in the South — though we don't yet know the sex of the child. After many weeks of conversation, Barb wanders into the living room one afternoon and says, "I feel so good about this birth mom, I feel like this is our child even if it's a boy. But if you don't feel the same, we can say no, if her ultrasound shows a boy." I meditate on this, and what comes through as clear as a bell is that we are to say yes to this child, whether it be a boy, girl, or twins — which at one point seems like is the case. The ultrasound confirms that it's just one child — a boy.

The situation of our second birth mother is nearly identical to that of our first one. Both of these young women want to go on with their education. Both are 18 at the birth of their second child and are already raising one child. Both were taught in their public schools that birth control pills will kill them, so they used nothing and got pregnant. Both come from very poor families and are thrilled their children will be able to learn about computers in our family.

Not everyone we know is happy about our choice to adopt again. We have African-American friends who totally support a white family adopting Black children. But we have others who have great reservations. Some even see our actions as destructive to African-American families and communities.

We don't see ourselves as heroes or bad guys. It's a situation fraught with contradiction and complexity, and in our view does not lend itself to simple answers. What is true is that for many reasons the children we are adopting cannot be reared in their birth families: There isn't enough money or support to make that happen. Many Black children end up in a huge pool of "hard to place" kids waiting for adoption and never find permanent homes outside an institution.

These children need a home, and we want to provide one. Ideally this should happen in their birth families, but that it happen somewhere is what we believe is most important.

A Dramatic Arrival

BARB

In late December 1989, we get a call that our son is on the way and I jump on a plane for one of our most southern states. Three days later I am holed up with Stephen in a motel in a small town in the swamps. We have to live here for a week to prove to the state that I am not kidnapping the child. The nurses from the hospital are great — they give me supplies and call every day to check on us — and the motel staff are wonderful too. But I'm nervous because I'm white and my baby is Black. Having grown up around here, I know I am doing something many people hate, and I know lots of scary stories about bodies that have disappeared in these parts. I am unable to shake my fear.

One afternoon I am holding the baby while I check my voicemail at work. Suddenly there's a tremendous roar outside and I spot a helicopter landing just outside my room. Armed men hop out. I am sure we are about to be assaulted and killed. I hang up the phone, rush into the bathroom with the baby, and lock the door. I wait, my fingers ready to dial 911, though help probably won't arrive in time.

An hour passes. Nothing happens. Then I hear the helicopter again. I leave the bathroom and look out the window. They're gone. I call the front desk, but no one knows who these people were, why they came, or why they left. "Probably a training exercise" is all anyone can figure out.

Could that be true? I sit with my new son, marveling that the world may have changed so much that my Black son and I are a nonevent. With that thought, I realize how much I have dreaded this trip, how afraid I've been, how completely I've surrendered to the possibility that we could be killed. And how prejudiced I am about the South.

The whole time I've been here, I've been surrounded by love and support, but I keep feeling like I am being stalked by a great lumbering presence on my left side, just out of view. I know on some level it's related to the lynchings, rapes and murders that have been committed here, to the centuries of my people brutalizing my son's people.

So my fear — which has been huge, vivid, and visceral — is based on real experience. But that experience is in the past. There is nothing in the current situation to support it. I have got to let go, open up, be present to possibility. This is the dawning of an ongoing and sometimes losing, often winning struggle for me.

Our Family Is Complete

STACY

Barb comes off the plane holding a warmly wrapped little bundle who is our son, Stephen. He is absolutely beautiful with huge gorgeous eyes and full lips. My heart melts. I look into his eyes and it feels like we've known each other forever.

So in Barb's and my thirteenth year together, our family is complete. We four somehow make a complete whole. It feels right. The only real regret we will have about Shawna and Stephen's babyhood is that we couldn't take more time off from work. We would have liked to have savored that time more. Also, as comparatively older parents (40 and 42 when Shawna arrived, 42 and 44 when we got Stephen), we were exhausted and could have used the rest! However, both adoptions cost more than we'd saved for them, and we were afraid of our new financial responsibilities.

Neither Barb nor I know what it is to have biological children. We've heard people talk about the bond that formed both before their kids came and after they were born. We wondered if being an adoptive parent would feel different. We can say without a single doubt that our maternal bonding with Stephen and Shawna happened immediately, powerfully, and irrevocably. We can't imagine how we could love any biological children more than we love these two human beings. Our fierce maternal love and protectiveness for these two children were there from Day One.

Like the Energizer Bunny

STACY

As an infant, Stephen is much more docile than Shawna was. If he's hungry, he lets out a peep and patiently waits for his bottle. Then something very interesting happens. The moment Stephen begins crawling, he becomes a different kid. It is amazing to watch. Suddenly it's like he has a little motor running in him, and he is off! As the months go by, this level of energy doesn't just continue, it grows. By the time he's walking, it's a full-time job just keeping up with him. Stephen has put new meaning into the word active!

Foxy Little Lady

BARB

The baby years roll by and soon Shawna is in preschool. Each June, the school holds a graduation ceremony for the kids heading to kindergarten. We all get dressed up and attend.

The parents look on in delight at the tiny children decked out in their best: the little boys in miniature suits, the little girls in dresses and bright hair ribbons. We're complimenting each other on our kids. The boys are "handsome," "darling," and "cute." The girls are "beautiful," "darling," and "cute." Except ... two different people come up and tell us that our daughter is "one foxy little lady."

Foxy? Is this an appropriate way to describe a 4-year-old? Is it because she's Black and adorable? Or because the only Black females they've seen are the hyper-sexualized images in the media? Why aren't they sexualizing the little white girls? Why are they sexualizing any little girl?

Even standing in the heat of the June sun, a chill shivers up my spine.

What's Hair Got to Do With It? Part 1

BARB

I am having an argument with Auntie Janine. She keeps her hair very short. In fact, she gets it cut very close at a barber shop. Shawna, now age 4, also wears her hair very short, and although she has pierced ears and wears earrings, we keep getting asked, "Oh, how old is *he*?"

Auntie Janine says, "You can't let her wear her hair like that. It isn't acceptable in the African-American community, and she's going to get teased. You should let it grow and braid it."

I argue back, "Why should we do that? Her hair is so gorgeous the way it is, thick and rich. Besides, you wear your hair short."

"That's different. It's more acceptable for an adult woman."

Months later, I'm in a grocery store. Shawna is with me. Her hair is now in dreads. An African-American woman walks up to me and says, "Don't you know a good hairstylist? I have one who can do great braids." I'm taken aback. I have never met this woman. I say that I really like my daughter's hair in dreads, it's why I learned how to do them. The woman shrugs and walks off.

A good friend of Stacy's, who's African-American, has her hair braided every six weeks. It takes 14 hours and costs $450. Her husband doesn't like it short or natural.

Once again I'm at the hairdressers with my daughter. Though we love her beautiful hair the way it is, we bow to the mounting criticism from Black women friends and the people on the street who think she's a boy. We're going to have it combed out, braided in cornrows against her scalp, and then add extensions so she has something to toss about. In order for this transformation to occur, Shawna has to have her hair straightened with a kind of reverse permanent, full of bad chemicals, then combed out. As the hair stylist proceeds, she is yanking Shawna's hair and Shawna starts crying.

"Stop, please stop" she pleads.

The African-American hair stylist, a beautiful woman who initially Shawna warmed up to, says, "Now, Shawna you don't want to look ugly with this nappy old head, do you?"

We shrink inside to think these are the options: go through agony to turn her hair into something very different than what she was born with, or look ugly and inappropriate in Black culture. What on earth are we as her parents to do?

Dummy Down, Drug 'Em Up, Part 1

BARB

When Stephen is 2, he is in for a regular medical check-up. As usual, he's opening drawers, sitting on the scale, hopping and skipping in the small room, singing and pretending to paint the walls with his fingers. The doctor comes in and pauses for a minute and then says, "You may be dealing with Attention Deficit Hyperactive Disorder. This looks like a pretty classic case."

I go home stunned, call Stacy at work to give her this bad news, and call several friends who are dealing with this condition in their kids. It sounds grim. One boy is now in a special school and the other drugged almost comatose each day. Another little girl regularly sees a psychiatrist — at age 4! I research the condition and find that Black boys are diagnosed with it 10 to 20 times more frequently than white boys are.

We decide to drop the whole hot potato for the moment.

Out of the Mouths of Babes

BARB

Shawna and I are taking a walk, her little black hand in my white one. She's 4.

We see a seagull circling around a tree full of crows, which are much smaller than the gull. I say to my daughter, "What do you think that seagull is doing, circling around and around like that?"

"She's telling her babies everything is okay, Mommy."

"But honey, a white bird can't have black—"

I stop myself.

"Yes, love, I think you're right. I think that's exactly what she's doing."

I marvel at the miracle of American family. This little girl could not even have been my friend, much less my daughter, growing up in the fifties. Now, many struggles but only a few decades later, she is my beloved daughter.

'What Did You Expect?'

BARB

I am watching the lights go out in our daughter's sparkling eyes in kindergarten, her first year in public school. Shawna loved preschool and was a leader. She has so much looked forward to "big school." And now this?

We can't figure it out. Her teacher is good; the school recommended her as one of their best. Yet this child, so lively at home, clams up and gets nearly catatonic in the classroom. Even though there isn't much asked of her, she seems scared. What's going on?

I have a conversation with the teacher, a very gifted woman with a terrific reputation and a master's degree in education.

"Do you know what might be going on with Shawna?"

She looks at me and without hesitating says, "Well, what did you expect?"

I'm really confused and starting to get scared. I ask her what she means.

Lowering her voice in a conciliatory tone, she leans towards me and says, "Was her mother on drugs? You know, she's adopted, she's got to be a crack baby, right?" The teacher cautions me not to expect Shawna to achieve much in school.

I close the conversation quickly, vowing to get our daughter out of this classroom as soon as possible. I don't want Shawna to be the victim of this teacher's assumption that adopted Black children are all drug babies and are therefore brain damaged. (Not all babies born to drug addicts are brain damaged. In fact, research demonstrates that the "drug" causing the most damage to babies is alcohol.)

Don't *expect* much? Talk about a self-fulfilling prophecy.

Stacy and I start talking with parents of other adopted and Black children, and soon have a support group going. We discover the powerful and crippling assumptions some people have about our children, assumptions that will later help us understand "the dimming of the lights" phenomenon in so many children of color.[2]

Francesca and Food

STACY

Amidst the difficulties, the blessings. Our next-door neighbor, Francesca, worries us. An Italian-American who grew up in this then rural (now urban) area where her father was a fruit picker, she seems racist and homophobic. Using every slur in the books, she doesn't like the Chinese who used to live in our house, and when

---

[2] If you doubt the influence of teachers and other school staff on children's opinions of each other, check out Jane Elliot's famous "Blue Eyes, Brown Eyes" exercise where white students are labeled inferior or superior based solely upon the color of their eyes and are thus exposed to the experience of being a minority. Fascinating — and frightening. And it certainly bears out our own experience with the effect of the expectations of teachers on the performance of their students.

she talks about Mexicans or gays, she uses all the words we associate with hatred and prejudice.

On the other hand, she is a special blessing in our life because she starts coming over to our house with fabulous homemade Italian food: spaghetti, pheasant and polenta, minestrone soup, her own cured olives. Just when we get home from work exhausted, having picked up the kids from school or childcare, there's a knock at the door. There Francesca stands, pot in hand. We are so exhausted, hungry and grateful, we often burst into tears.

Over time, we realize that Francesca is *not* prejudiced in the ways we were thinking, despite her language. Despite her words for gays, she is feeding us every night and knits baby clothes for us. It turns out that the "C****" (bad-word for Chinese-American) down the street is one of her best friends, she adores the "S***" (Mexican) couple across the street and house-sits when they are out of the country, and she really appreciates how the "F****s" (gay men) down the block are lifting up the whole neighborhood with their home renovation.

But we also find, as our friendship with her deepens, that Francesca becomes softer and even more open to people different from herself, including all our friends. This phenomenon is one we observe in others as well. It seems like when a person has positive experiences with someone from the particular group of people they don't like, their prejudice shifts to more of a tolerance, sometimes even to acceptance. Making someone the "enemy" becomes much harder when you share food.

It strikes us that the only way to completely dehumanize others is to demonize them, and that requires keeping great distance. This is because connecting with the enemy, seeing them as fellow parents who love their kids, for example, makes waging war against them much more difficult. Sam Keen writes about the requirement in war of demonizing the "enemy" in *Faces of the Enemy.*[3]

I think our family is helping Francesca to see the world a little differently and she is helping us keep warm and fed. She's also taught us to look beyond the language a person uses and into their eyes and hearts. (Some of the nicest-sounding words are spoken with the cold mean eyes of so-called liberals!)

Inside vs. Outside

STACY

As the kids grow, we often feel like we're trudging through a dense forest with a machete. No path has been laid, no compass is available. We vacillate between feeling like what we are doing is what needs to happen in the world and feeling like idiots. On the one hand, we feel like we are contributing to humanity's preservation. On the other, we suspect we are fools for having taken on a challenge that could kill all four of us.

Inside our home all we're doing is trying to raise two kids, and together we're four humans who love each other, like each other (most of the time), and really enjoy each other's company. But more and more, as the kids emerge into the world and out of the safety and protection of our closed home environment, things start happening that tell

---

[3] *Faces of the Enemy: Reflections of the Hostile Imagination* by Sam Keen, HarperCollins, 1991

us no matter how normal we think we are or want to be, much of the world has others things to say.

A Visit From Child Protective Services

BARB

I am at work with a $5,000-a-day consultant when my pager goes off. I run to a phone and call the number. It's where Stephen is in aftercare.

Annie, the caregiver, says, "Something terrible has happened. You've got to come right away."

"Is he hurt?" I ask.

"No ..."

"Well, did he hurt someone else?"

"Not exactly. You've got to come right now."

"Okay, okay, I'm on my way." I blow off the consultant and all that money, and race off. I'm so scared I can hardly drive. I get to the house and knock on the door. It's a dark day and there are no lights on in the house. Annie comes to the door looking white as a sheet. Behind her in the gloom stands my dear boy, a worried look on his face.

"Mommy, is it night time? What time is it? Mommy, pick me up."

I gather him up and we go to the kitchen with Annie.

"You son has initiated my son into the ways of evil," she says.

"What?" I ask, incredulous.

"I found him and Tommy in the closet with their pants down looking at each other."

"Oh, Annie, that behavior is epidemic right now at Stephen's nursery school. They say it's completely normal and will pass. We're all talking about it, and telling the kids to zip it up and get back to the Play-Doh. The teachers have assured us it happens every year and the worst thing we can do is make a big deal out of it."

"I can't have him back here. I've packed up all his things. You should go now. Everything is by the door."

This is the last time we see Annie, who has cared for our son after preschool since he was a baby. We never see her husband, Jim, again either: Jim, who Stephen has called "daddy," to everyone's delight. For the next year, Stephen will ask about his friend Tommy and daddy Jim and Annie.

Two days after this incident, we get an urgent call from Children's Protective Services. It seems someone whom they can't name has reported us as unfit parents, and would like us investigated because we have encouraged our son's "sexual perversity."

The social worker shows up with only twenty minutes' warning. We are very nervous. He's African-American. I think, *Is he one of the many social workers who think we're contributing to genocide by adopting our son in the first place?*

We talk for three hours. To our enormous relief, after telling this man our version of the incident, as well as detailing other experiences we've had as the mothers of a Black son, he says the call has made him mad.

35

"I have so many calls to deal with where there *is* really something going on." He puts his arms around us, says, "God bless you women," and walks out.

This is the beginning of our recognizing a pattern in which white people see our Black children as oversexed, a stereotyping of Black men and women that apparently begins in preschool. I recall darling little Shawna in her dress-up outfit being called "a foxy little lady."

It's also another case of assumptions, like the assumption that Shawna was a crack baby and therefore would never learn. This time the assumption is that there are no Black boys, really. There are only Black men, just little. They are already rapists and murderers and should be punished now, while we've still got them.

What is really going on behind this stereotype and these assumptions? And how do we break through them? We wonder if our being lesbians catalyzes the sexual perversity agenda, but when we talk to other parents of Black boys, parents who are heterosexual, we find it's happened to their kids, too.

Evil vs. Naughty

BARB

It's boiling hot and I'm dripping wet, although it's only 10 o'clock in the morning. With our friend Sally, Stacy and I are here at preschool to "observe" (a.k.a. police) our 3-year-old sons during the morning break. This is our fifth day and so far the boys have done nothing different than the other kids. They have been reprimanded like the others when they've pushed too hard, or yelled too loud, or forgotten to turn off the water. Like us, Sally and Tom are Caucasian. Like our kids, Sally and Tom's kids are adopted. They are also racially mixed. Unlike ours, their kids look white.

"Have you noticed how they talk to you about your son compared to how they talk to us about ours?" Sally asks.

"What do you mean?" I ask, feeling a creeping dread — she's about to point out something I'm trying mightily not to see.

"Well, they're all hysterical about your boy, grave concerns, big worries, wondering if he's seen a doctor, if he needs medications before something really bad happens. And when they talk to us about our son, who's doing the exact same things Stephen is — let's face it, we've seen them together when they play at our houses and we've been watching them here for a week, the boys are identical except for their skin color — they laugh and say our son is full of beans and we've got to keep an eye on him. It's like your son's behavior is evil and our son's identical behavior is just naughty."

Sally's words illuminate the invisible stage that's been set for our son's years to come in our predominantly white neighborhoods: Black kids are considered dangerous, no matter how young.

We're so grateful we have friends like Sally and Tom to help us navigate the waters. Without allies like them, we would not make it through. Tom is a lawyer and will be our advocate with the police and the district attorney in the years to come.

Dummy Down, Drug 'Em Up, Part 2

BARB

Stephen is 3. He's more active than ever and is growing in leaps and bounds. Three months ago he was a size four. Now he's a size eight. Unfortunately, he's been asked to leave two daycares for refusing to follow directions, sit quietly on a carpet square during story time, nap quietly in the afternoon. We are now at his third school and are told he will have to leave unless we medicate him. Recently he used a plastic plate from the play kitchen as a Frisbee. The teacher assures us many families find Ritalin to be a great solution.

We try it. Stephen calms down, way down. In fact, he's practically comatose and has stopped eating. The daycare raves about the difference and marvels at the art he now produces, focused intently on paints and paper. We are uneasy. It seems the light has gone out of his eyes, and sometimes you have to call him three times before he snaps out of his daze long enough to answer. The tension builds: The teachers are thrilled with the way Stephen can stay focused; we respond, "Yes, but his *spirit* is gone."

We take him off the Ritalin and move to the fourth daycare. Soon we get the ultimatum: meds or out. Since we're both working full-time jobs, we decide to try another medication that supposedly avoids the side effects of Ritalin. It works okay, but now we notice that we're inducing a manic-depressive roller coaster ride in our son every day. He wakes up off the wall, full of energy, racing around the house. We give him his pill and he falls into a pit of low energy and intense close-up focus, climbing slowly out of the pit as the medication wears off around noon — by which time he's off the wall again, takes another pill and plummets. Unless one of us can leave work to pick Stephen up at 4 when the lunch pill wears off, one more cycle occurs before the poor kid hits his bed for the night.

In the middle of all this, we go to a Club Med in Mexico — a break ordered by Barb's therapist very concerned at how stressed out she is — where they have lots of cool activities for kids (and where parents get a real vacation.). Our son is still on medication, and we explain the medical regimen to the young guy running the program. He says, "Nah, don't give him meds. My little brother's exactly like him. If he gets too antsy, I'll just let him run or swim. He'll be fine here." And sure enough, we take Stephen off the meds and he does great. He swims in the pool or the ocean from eight in the morning until ten at night.

Once we're back home, we decide to lie. It seems to us by far the lesser of two evils and an example of the "situational ethics" we both studied in theology classes years ago. We tell the teacher Stephen's on a new medicine and doing great. The first day back, we go to pick up our son and the teacher says,

"Wow, I didn't realize that there wasn't much light in his eyes before. He's so *present* now."

End of the story with meds. Whenever they insist in the future, we'll just assure them we'll comply.

Here's another one of those assumptions that are making our son's life so difficult: Children (of any color) who won't sit on a carpet square and listen quietly to a story for half an hour should be medicated. Fifteen minutes of recess is sufficient for an active, growing child; any hyperactivity after that fifteen minutes is proof that medication is necessary.

It seems to us that somehow in our country, we've organized life to work only if someone in the mix is drugged. During the "Ozzie and Harriet," "Leave it to Beaver," and "Father Knows Best" years, it was the women who were drugged. Lots of Valium and all the ensuing consequences, including addiction, despair, and in the case of the mother of one of my best friends in high school, suicide. Now, because so many women have to work, the kids are drugged. Where is this coming from? The advertising of the drug companies? The American dream of being happy all the time? Why is the United States the largest consumer of these kinds of "controlling behavior" drugs?

People we've talked to who have either been born in or lived in other cultures share with us the ways they have been able to deal with very active children. For instance, in Germany, music labs have been created where kids can play drums to their hearts' content, resulting in a decrease of anxiety and an increase in calm. In India, many classes are held under the trees and the "over-active" kids run around the tree until they can sit still. The best book we've read on this issue talks about hunters in a farmer's world. Some kids, like our Stephen, have the skills of a hunter's culture: hypervigilance, noticing any little change in patterns around them, always ready to run, jump, and hit or throw for food and for safety. And then, exhausted, they go home as warriors to eat and rest.

What if we decided, as a country, to get off drugs? What kind of pedagogies would develop? How would they benefit all kids? What might happen with our imaginations, our families, and our communities if we stopped taking drugs and developed other ways of dealing with how we feel and act without them?

God's Will

STACY

I'm in Greece with my mom and aunt visiting my 90-year-old grandmother, who is in a nursing home. I've adored my Nana all my life. I carry her name, Anastasia, and as the first-born grandchild, I've been doted on by her and by my grandfather.

It's very hard seeing my Nana in this nursing home, and I'm feeling scared and vulnerable. Although her face lights up when I come into the room, she doesn't recognize me well enough to call me by name.

After a couple of intense days, my mom, aunt, and I decide to take a day-long cruise to visit a couple of islands that are close by. We get off at the first island and go down to a beach to relax a little. The gorgeous water beckons and my 80-year-old aunt and I go in for swim. I'm feeling more relaxed than I've been in a while.

Out of nowhere, my aunt says, "Can I ask you something?"

Bathing in the cobalt blue Mediterranean Sea off the island of Hydra in Greece, I figure I can probably answer any question here. I say okay.

She asks, "Why Black kids? Why did you adopt Black kids?"

I feel my whole body tense up, thinking of my kids, now 6 and 3. "Well, why not?" I respond. "Why are you asking me this?"

She says, "Well, it's a double whammy for your mother. First you being gay and then adopting Black kids. It would have been easier if you'd adopted an Oriental baby, or even Mexican."

First, I want to correct her and say, Asian, not Oriental. Instead I say, "Black, Asian, Mexican, we were open to any child who wasn't white because only the white ones are guaranteed to be adopted." The conversation has triggered in me defensiveness and rage at the virulence of racism directed at Black people in the U.S., a country that they basically settled, long before Greeks and many other ethnicities even arrived.

But is this reaction appropriate? Is this beloved aunt really being virulently racist? I deeply love her. I grew up with her; she was my second mother. And she's one of the few people I know who really works hard at not being judgmental. I have been able to pause long enough to realize that these questions she's asking are coming more from a place of genuine inquiry than judgment.

Letting the warm, gentle Mediterranean Sea rock me and wash away my initial irritation and anger, I go on to say that this life I have created is the life I want. In fact, it feels meant to be. It represents who I truly am. And part of my life is to have adopted Black children, particularly because they are not usually the first children to be adopted.

She says, "Well, I did say to your mother that it's God's will."

I tell her that's exactly how I experience the miracle of our family. God's will.

We finish our bathing and go onto the beach to enjoy fresh fried calamari. Still, the great food and bright sun don't completely dispel the deep sadness and mild dread my aunt's questions and my initial reaction have inspired in me.

'What If Her's Not a Brown Girl?'

BARB

We're at the dining room table eating our pb & j. Shawna, now 6, cries out at Stephen, "Stop staring at me!"

Stephen, who's 4, immediately tears up. "I not staring at you!"

I jump in. "Stephen, your eyes are so big and beautiful that people think you're staring when you're just looking. You're just looking at Shawna, but she thinks you're staring at her."

Shawna calms down. Stephen looks at me, big brown eyes full of questions.

"But," I continue, "someday there will be a girl that will love that you look at her with your big beautiful brown eyes."

"What's her name?" Stephen asks.

"Well, we don't know her name yet. You have to grow up a little more, and then she'll come into your life. And she'll love you looking at her, and you'll love her and look at her all the time."

"But what if her's not a brown girl?" he asks.

Oh my God, I think, *does he already know this could be a problem? At age 4?* And I comfort myself with the thought of how far things have come since I was 4 years old — may the miracle continue to unfold! Quickly!

Making Music

STACY

Stephen is now graduating from the same nursery school that Shawna attended. I've volunteered to write a song about the school. My friend and vocal coach and I sing it.

Barb and I love this school, with ten languages, kids of every skin color, and spots reserved for homeless children that the rest of us help pay for. It's a gorgeous sunny day and when I look out at all the faces, including the faces of my children, I experience joy and a deep feeling of peace. This is one of those wonderful moments when God's in His/Her heaven and all's right with the world. In microcosm, it's an American family for all God's children. As a two-mom family, we are held in a loving and diverse community that supports all of us. Our children are seen as what they are: simply children.

The Miracle of Gina

BARB

The unrelenting physical and mental Olympics of these early years are relieved by the miracle of Gina. We meet her before we adopt, and once the kids are with us and we are suffering from intense sleep deprivation, Gina often magically appears and swoops the kids away to the park, to the children's museum, for a walk. People where she takes the kids assume she is their grandmother, to her (and our) delight.

Our gratitude and relief are immeasurable. Gina asks nothing in return. Ever. Having had four children of her own, she knows what is required and does it. She's really our only back-up as we raise our kids, go to work, and occasionally grab a few moments for ourselves.

One of our great losses occurs when the kids are 4 and 6, and Gina leaves the area to move in with her grown kids and her new grandchildren as a full-time, fully satisfied nanny-grandmother. (As a mom, Gina lost custody of her children when she came out as a lesbian; her husband sought and won exclusive custody.) She remains in our lives to this day, whenever we can get together.

Moving Up

STACY

Shawna is in first grade and has been sent to "Resource" to get extra help — her reading progress isn't moving along as it should. The Resource teacher is wonderful and is African-American, so there is nothing going on but the fact of Shawna's lack of progress. As our parent special-ed meetings with her continue, she tells us that Shawna is going to need a lot more help than our wonderful, racially mixed district can provide. She says the best school district for what our daughter will need is one farther north, and if there is any way we can afford to live there, we should move.

"But what about racial diversity? That town is so white!" we counter.

The Resource teacher says that we need to get Shawna's academics solid first, because nothing will make up for that not being right. And we can bring more Black kids into Shawna's life through after school programs and friends.

So, through extraordinary advocacy from friends and a principal in the new town, we move into a perfect school in the middle of Shawna's first-grade year. There are farm animals on the playground, an organic garden, teacher/student ratios the best in the state, and a principal intent on diversifying the almost all-white school by proactively recruiting transfers from the poor town nearby.

Stephen is in a new preschool. We rent for a while and then finally buy a house that's so run down we can almost afford it, and we're set.

'Mommy, I Want to Die'

STACY

It's bedtime two months later. Stephen has just turned 5 and I am in his room to tuck him in and kiss him goodnight. He has had a rough day at school, and as he turns his head toward me, I see tears streaming down his face.

I ask him why he's crying.

"I want to die, Mommy, I don't want to be brown anymore." He is in that place between waking and sleep, and his words and feelings are without guile, drama, or defense.

I feel like someone has just stabbed me in the heart. I can barely breathe. I say, "Sweetie, what happened today? Did something happen to make you feel bad?"

He looks at me and says, "I don't want to be brown."

This feels like more than just an incident. It feels bigger, like it is wrenched out of his being when he's falling asleep and wide open. I sit and stroke his head until he falls asleep, tears now in my eyes too. Everything in my chest and stomach feels knotted and I hurt. Unbidden, the song "Suicide is Painless" from the TV show "M*A*S*H" starts playing in my head. No coincidence. The program is about the Korean War, when the will to survive sits alongside the need to escape from the terror of war. I think, *This is just a different kind of war.*

When Stephen finally falls asleep, I go to tell Barbara what has happened, but I can hardly find my voice. Our son is talking about wanting to die at the age of 5. And that wish is for him connected to the color of his skin.

I will remember and relive this evening, these words, and the feeling in my body again and again in the coming years. Whenever I share this story, others cry, even some of those who think there's no race problem in America. The poignancy and depth of our boy's pain is recognized by all who hear it.

Why do we need "proof" and "statistics" to point to the ravages and devastation of racism, or any other form of oppression, when we have these kinds of stories? All we need is the intention, the commitment to individually, societally, and globally stop doing whatever makes a little boy say such a thing.

'Get That Boy Under Control Before The Man Does ...'

BARB

We're at Auntie Janine's and Uncle Juan's for Christmas day. We do a lot of holidays together, and both kids have spent weekends there without us. We are very focused on raising them to be bi-cultural, at home in either Black or white settings. Obviously we can't be around if they are to acculturate in all-Black settings. For this holiday, we're together, racially mixed, as extended family.

Stephen is 5 years old. He's at a stage where his hands don't stop grabbing and his arms don't stop swinging. At some point, he picks up a glass candy dish, whirls it around, and throws it. Glass and candy fly everywhere.

Janine, normally calm and collected, starts screaming hysterically, "You got to get that boy under control before The Man does it for you. He's going to be another Rodney King if you don't get him under control!"

We look at her, shocked. We've never seen Janine like this. She is so emotional and vehement today, a contrast from her usual calm and serene demeanor.

A few minutes later she's telling us how she's taking the next day off to go get Juan's driver's license renewed. It expired a few days ago and she can't sleep for worrying that he'll be stopped, and then things could escalate and she'll be getting a call that her husband's dead. This is a vice-president at a major Fortune 100 company, taking the day off to get her husband's driver's license renewed for fear he'll be killed if she doesn't.

We know about the statistical reality of how dangerous it is for Black and brown men to encounter police. But this isn't some impartial conversation or article on statistics and racial profiling. These are our friends, Janine and Juan, and their day-to-day lives. This is about their fear for our son. They are taking us inside a world that most white people never experience firsthand.

And now because we've entered that world through our children, we see and experience a reality that chills us to the bone. This is no longer just interesting or informative dinner conversation. It's life and death — and we're terrified for our children.

Thank God for Good Teachers

STACY

Shawna has a wonderful, compassionate, and gifted first-grade teacher who does something that has not happened before. She fully recognizes our daughter's gifts and puts them to use in the classroom. Rather than focusing on Shawna's dyslexia, she makes her a helper, asking her to gather materials and pass them out to other students, among other tasks. Shawna flourishes under this teacher's care.

When the school term ends, the teacher asks if Shawna would come back in the fall and help her sometimes in the second-grade classroom. Shawna does and our hearts are full to see how this helps our daughter keep her confidence up. Every day in second grade she must attend special reading classes, and she struggles with numbers and letters, words and simple sentences. Shawna hates being singled out as different, and made to attend special classes.

Her former teacher reassures her day in and day out, "You are a natural teacher. You do better with a room of 5-year-olds than I do, and I've had twenty years' experience! Please promise me you'll come back and do your teaching internship with me when you go on to become a teacher!"

Shawna basks in this vision of herself and plows on through the daily grind of learning despite a heavy handicap.

N****s in the Pool

BARB

It's summer and I'm at the neighborhood association's pool with our son, 5, and our daughter, who's just turned 8. While they're swimming and playing, I overhear a conversation between three little white girls, aged about 7 or 8.

"Look, there's n****s in the pool," one of them says.

Because I'm white, they don't know I'm the mother of those "n****s." I go over to them and say, "I heard what you said about my kids. Please don't ever say that again. That word is very hurtful and it's not okay to use it."

They look surprised and swim away from me.

Now I'm at my son's soccer game talking with one of the moms who also belongs to the association's pool. We're talking about our kids and some of the challenges we face, and I mention the incident at the pool.

This woman, a good and reasonable woman in my experience, looks at me and says, "Oh that couldn't have happened at our pool!"

I look right back at her and say, "But it did happen. This isn't a rumor. I heard it with my own two ears."

She responds with a vague "Oh, I just really can't believe that ..." and a few seconds later she drifts away.

How do we deal with "Oh" and "That doesn't happen here" and "This is such a liberal community, we're so lucky"? Isn't this really more difficult than dealing with those who will use the "n" word to your face? The diffuse, elusive denial and fear of good people ... how can we find ways to enter into those areas together and talk about what's really going on?

How can I raise the issue and not have people swim or otherwise drift away from me? How can I not come across as so righteous that they feel judged — especially when I *am* judging them and coming across with off-putting urgency out of terror for my kids?

Kindness in the Schoolroom?

BARB

Stephen's just started kindergarten at the local elementary school. We're thrilled with his teacher, who is young, bright and full of energy. She's just finished her Ph.D. for her study of "Kindness in the Schoolroom," and our first two meetings are great stories of Stephen's progress.

And then comes the afternoon when she calls to tell us that if she believed in the devil, she would say Stephen was possessed. He was grabbing food from other children and stepping on their toes if they didn't hand it over.

We ask her what she did about it and she says she can do nothing when a child acts this way. We ask her what Stephen had to say for himself and she says she never asked.

We ask Stephen — who's been home from school for about an hour — what on earth was going on. He bursts into tears and says that someone had stolen his lunch and snack tickets, and he was "starving to death" and grabbing food from other kids was the only way he could get food.

We call the teacher back and give her Stephen's side of the story. She responds, "That's ridiculous. I saw those lunch tickets. He had lunch tickets."

I ask her if she's actually seen them turn into food, and Stephen eating. She explains that she doesn't go into the lunchroom but she is sure he's eaten. We remind her how important it is that he eat, given that he has hypoglycemia.

We call the principal to explain that one of us will accompany Stephen to class until a meeting with him, the teacher, us and the school psychologist can be arranged.

The next day I go in with Stephen. His teacher comes to me with a lunch and a snack ticket: A mother has called after she found them in her child's lunch box, and the child confessed to her he'd stolen them out of Stephen's lunchbox. The teacher does not apologize or say anything at all to Stephen or me about her own behavior.

The principal is sufficiently disturbed by our story, which the teacher corroborates, that he immediately transfers Stephen out of the classroom into a new class. The rest of the year proceeds without incident. The new teacher is wonderful.

The first teacher has a few more unfortunate experiences with other parents and resigns before the end of the year. We are deeply saddened by this. What did this young, bright, enthusiastic and committed teacher need that she didn't get in the way of coaching and guidance? What if we had been able to be less freaked out and more helpful?

Our new teacher completes the year but then decides to transfer to another school. At her invitation, and with the support of the principal, we follow. We have already learned that it is the rare Caucasian teacher who can handle a big Black boy who is very active and verbal as if he's his age (this year, just 5) and just a kid, not a budding criminal or the devil incarnate. We wish we knew how to go after this huge issue more effectively, but for now, we need to get our own Black boy educated and that's taking every ounce of energy we have.

'He Has a Violent Look in His Eyes'

BARB

Our son is 5, in an aftercare school program for first grade. We dread the week of the O.J. Simpson verdict, since whenever a prominent African-American male is apprehended, our son experiences subtle or overt targeting. Wonderfully, the week proceeds without incident. By Friday morning, we believe we are home free.

But Friday afternoon we are both paged at work and asked to leave immediately and come to the aftercare program. Once there we are handed paperwork stating there will be no violence at the center. We say, of course not, and ask, has Stephen done anything violent? No. Had anyone done something violent to Stephen? No. *What is the problem?* We ask.

"He has a violent look in his eyes," the director of the program tells us.

We protest, but move on. "Is everything else okay?" we ask.

"Yes, Stephen has many friends and is seen as a leader."

"Oh yes," we say, "and there's one little girl that he seems to play with a lot."

"Well," the director says, "that is a big problem because they have had sex talk in the bushes."

We ask what the staff did after discovering Stephen and the little girl in this situation. The staff said they didn't know what to do. We ask what they do in other cases where this happens.

"Well," says the director, "normally they tell the children it is inappropriate and ask them not to do it again."

We wonder aloud why the situation with our son is not a "normal" situation, and ask that they follow their normal process with Stephen and the little girl. We assure them that we will discuss this with our son, too.

When we talk about this situation with Stephen, he says the little girl chases boys, even into the boys' restroom where she pulls down their pants and threatens them with her older brother (who we learn later doesn't even exist).

Over the weekend, we check with other parents using the aftercare program and three of them corroborate Stephen's story. Their sons have also been chased into the boys' bathroom or into the bushes by this girl.

The following Monday, the director calls to say we need to come in again. This time we are served with a letter drafted by the aftercare lawyer saying that if Stephen ever has sex talk with this little girl again, he will be asked to leave. We ask the director to do two things before we will accept this letter: 1) Investigate what is going on with this child that she chases boys, pulls their pants down and initiates sex talk; and 2) Check with the lawyer to see whether a second letter to the parents of the only African-American child in the program is wise within 24 hours of the first letter, which was based solely on the "look in his eyes" of a 5-year-old.

There are no more incidents or letters during the days that pass before we withdraw Stephen from a program where he is obviously not wanted or respected, and where the staff is clearly targeting him and our family.

Brandishing Firearms

BARB

Our son's first-grade teacher at the local elementary school, who was carried over from kindergarten, is great. But life on the playground is another story. The kids are grossly under-supervised. There are two bizarre incidents, both on the playground, both handled by the principal.

In the first incident, Stephen, who has just turned 6, is suspended for "brandishing firearms." The firearm in question is a one-half-inch charm of a gun from his sister's souvenir bracelet from the Grand Canyon. (Stephen experiences strong consequences at home and never repeats this mistake.) Having taken care of business on the home front, our next stop is the principal, young, enthusiastic and in her first year in this new job.

We explain to her that we do not dispute the zero-tolerance policy, nor Stephen's suspension. What we're here to request is that she remove the suspension notice from his file. To create a paper trail on an African-American boy for "brandishing firearms" at age 5 is damning and potentially dangerous for him. The "firearm," after all, is from a charm bracelet. The principal refuses to remove the paperwork. We escalate the matter to the assistant superintendent of schools, who also refuses our request. We tell him that next we'll speak to the school board. He reluctantly removes the paperwork from Stephen's file.

No One Is Connecting the Dots

BARB

A few months later, the second incident occurs with Stephen at his elementary school, again on the mostly unsupervised playground. One of the little boys brings a match to the playground and, with three other little boys — including Stephen — digs a hole to build a "safe bonfire" of dead leaves, the way he learned in Cub Scouts. All four of these 5- and 6-year-old boys are suspended. All are African-American.

Obviously, building fires is very serious, and all the boys experience strong consequences at home. In the meantime, we raise the question to the young principal, "Why, when there are only four African-American boys in the whole kindergarten-first grade combined, are they all hanging out together? They don't even know each other from elsewhere. They aren't even in the same class or grade. Why aren't they part of the playgroups consisting of kids from their own classroom, like the other kids are? Don't they feel integrated into the white groups? Don't they feel safe?"

The principal neither understands our questions nor finds the phenomenon curious. When we point out that she's just suspended *all* the African-American 5- and 6-year-olds in those two grades, she counters that she does not see color — color has nothing to do with it.

At this point we escalate once again to the assistant superintendent of schools. We are not disputing the suspension, but the paper trail. Because Stephen's file will follow him throughout his school years and beyond, having paperwork in that file stating that as a 5- and then 6-year-old, this boy brought a gun to school and brandished it, or set the playground on fire (which the boys' small, contained fire did not) would only further cement the stereotype that he's a budding criminal. The assistant superintendent agrees to remove the paperwork on our son, but not on the other African-American boys unless their own parents come in and request it.

We point out that one of those boys is being raised by his grandmother, who works full-time at a job with no scheduling flexibility. She doesn't want a paper trail on her boy either, but she cannot come in for the process. The superintendent's assistant, who is a kind and mild-mannered Black man, explains that every child is treated as an individual, and they cannot transfer the remedy worked out with one family to another. It is up to each family to discuss their own situation.

From my past work as a civil-rights investigator, I recall and tell them about the rationale behind a decision in the famous civil rights case *Griggs vs. Duke Power* and point out that this policy of not extending the remedy for one child to others in the same "class" or category, while neutral on its face, has a disparate impact on kids whose parents don't know the system, don't speak the language, and/or can't get away from work — disproportionately kids of color. Therefore, it is a form of discrimination prohibited by civil rights law unless proven otherwise by the school district. The assistant superintendent refuses to budge. We do not have time to organize other parents of Black children, nor the time or money to catalyze a lawsuit in their behalf. The policy remains to this day.

The principal in charge during the "firearm" and "fire-starting" incidents resigns two years later citing "burn-out," and the young Black assistant superintendent dies of a heart attack just three years later. To us the loss of a bright and committed principal and the tragic early death of this young assistant both demonstrate that racism hurts everybody, not just its most immediate victims.

The Judging Machine

BARB

I'm standing in line waiting to order East Indian food at my neighborhood restaurant, for once not the only white person in the restaurant. In front of me is a white man who is wearing his gas station uniform. I think to myself, *What in the world is he doing here? He probably doesn't have a clue about Indian food.* Armed with my extensive knowledge and experience of Indian food, I initiate a conversation with him and start explaining how great the food is in this restaurant.

He warmly smiles at me and says, "Yeah, I'm married to an Indian woman and I've tasted all kinds of Indian food, but I haven't had the chance to try this restaurant yet."

I walk to the table to join my Indian friend and say, "Well, the joke is on me," as I share the experience. I am amazed at my own mind, how automatically it judges and categorizes in a nanosecond. And how completely wrongly. After suffering from the effects of people who do the same thing to my family! How can I still be like this? How does the miracle of the American family unfold, given how people are — including how I am, despite the best intentions?

My Nana's Memorial

STACY

It's the memorial service for my beloved grandmother, the one I am named after, the one who gave us my dowry by slipping it piece by piece into paper bags she handed to Barb whenever we came over to dinner. My Nana knew about Barb and me, obviously, but none of us ever spoke of it.

When my grandmother died, a part of me died with her. It was hard, too, that she died in Greece and I wasn't there. So I want to go to her memorial at my folks' church. With Barb. My parents are fine with Barb coming.

The morning of the service, Barb decides we should bring Shawna, 8, who says she really, really wants to go, but probably really, really just wants to skip school for a day. I am very alarmed because deep inside I know this will be a big problem for my family, but I don't say anything. Barb is waxing on with her logic: It will be perfect — a beautiful church, gorgeous music, a farewell to the great Nana that Shawna too has loved, and then Greek food, Shawna's favorite.

So we take Shawna with us. In the car on the way up to San Francisco, I explain my misgivings. Barb suggests we call my mother to tell her Shawna is coming. Mom is

upset, but she reluctantly agrees that we can bring
Shawna. After hanging up, I feel anxious about my mother,
her uncertainty, and the likely response of others. I call her
back. She tells me she is very upset Shawna is coming, and
embarrassed and ashamed of herself for her feelings, but
it is how she feels. She says she can't help it, it's her
background, the way she's been raised. She says she
doesn't know how she will explain Shawna to the Greek
community.

I say, "Nobody cares. The church has Black people
attending it already."

She says, "You're right. But it's protocol for only
immediate family members to sit in front. Could Barb and
Shawna sit somewhere else?" She's clearly struggling with
how to explain a white woman (which is how Greeks think
of white people who aren't Greek) and a Black child sitting
in the family section right next to me. I understand the
struggle. I grew up in this community and the backlash of
not following *to prepi* (the expected protocol) can be a
killer. But unlike Mom, I do have community outside this
closed system, so I don't have to worry about judgments
the way she has to.

Both Mom and I are struggling. I feel paralyzed. This is
a memorial for my grandmother, who I still miss terribly.
Should I not go to the memorial?

Barb turns to me and says, "Shawna and I will sit in the
back."

My heart is breaking.

During the service, I cry. For Nana, for my beloved Barb
and Shawna, my family, who aren't sitting with me. For the
pain we're all feeling. For what seems to be my own lack of

courage to stand up and say ... something. What, I'm not sure.

After the memorial, I cannot wait to leave. But my mom comes up and says, "I want you all to come to the reception."

I start crying. "No, we can't do this."

Mom's crying now too. "Please honey, come with Barb and Shawna. I'm so sorry."

Barb walks up, and Mom repeats her words to Barb. Now Barb is crying too. We really just want to go home, this whole thing has been completely exhausting. But both Mom and Shawna insist we go.

When we get to the reception, no one blinks an eye that we are there and Shawna is with us. Mom later confirms no one has said a thing to her about it.

Oddly, something profound shifts that day. As painful and difficult as this whole thing is, I discover that I'd rather deal with people — including my own family — who are honest about how they feel than with people who say, "Oh I have no biases," "Oh, that could never happen here!", "Oh, I don't see color, I'm color blind." The former is gritty, heartbreaking work, but the possibility for change occurs when people tell the truth. The other is a denial that is almost impossible to penetrate.

I know of no one without bias or prejudice of some kind. The majority of people walking around this planet have some version of prejudice. Call it being human, the air we breathe, or the environment we grow up in. It's present. In all of us. It's in me.

My mother adores Shawna. She's the only one who ever "gets it right" on the presents — the right toy when she is younger, the right purse or shoes or outfit when she's older. She has been willing to do the extremely difficult and painful work of looking at her own racism, to the point of being physically sickened by it. She tells the truth and I respect her for that. I think her truth telling and our ensuing conversations are what have allowed us to have an ever-deepening relationship as a family.

If two people are trying to have an open and honest conversation about issues of race (or any other topic involving diversity), where is the conversation going to go if one, or both, declare themselves color-blind, liberal, without bias? I'm not saying people don't believe their own words. In fact, that scares me most, that they *do* believe them.

Uncovering one's own unconsciousness on these issues can be terribly difficult and painful work. And it's also where the joy and possibility lie. If we can bring to light what is there, talk about that with honesty and humility, *then* we have a conversation worth having. Because in that moment we're creating a different world. We don't have to agree. Just talking about things as they really are transforms the current reality so something new and wonderful can emerge.

Shawna remembers the day of my grandmother's memorial as the time she could eat all the *spanakopita* she wanted, the time we parked right in the middle of the street in front of the church. She continually astonishes us with her "glass half-full" philosophy, choosing to remember only what serves her own view of the world: She is beloved, the world is her oyster, and happiness is the purpose of her own and everyone else's life.

PART II:
ELEMENTARY
AND MIDDLE SCHOOL

Two Introverts Trying to Build Community
STACY

Barb and I are both reclusive by nature. We're introverts. No one believes us when we say that because both of us seem outgoing. And we are, when we have to be. And sometimes we even want to be. But it's hard for us to reach out. And in that isolation, alone with our minds, things can get dicey. Loneliness and thought distortion are among the consequences.

We know from experience that the challenges in our lives are much less daunting when we engage with others and joy is augmented when we connect with others. Each time either or both of us have that experience, we remember how all of life is really about love and connection.

Then we forget again and are left with the company of our minds. The saying, "Don't go into your mind alone, it's a bad neighborhood," really applies.

So we practice. Practice getting out, having dinner with others, having people over, using the phone to connect. We laugh together often and say how much easier it would be if at least *one* of us were extroverted. Arranging a social event can be amazingly difficult. So practice is the order of the day.

We find that to build community involves patience, open-mindedness, and putting forth the energy that enables having experiences with others, even if those experiences are not always satisfying for us or others. That's part of it, like in any relationship.

Oh yeah, and if we want allies in our lives, it helps if we know one another. That may sound ridiculously simple. Yet, it's easy for us to forget. So, practice, practice, and more practice. Like the 12-step programs say, it's progress not perfection (thank God).

Ongoing Support on the Home Front
BARB

My younger sister, Maggie, is determined that we move to North Carolina. She can't bear the tales we regale her with of life in our so-called liberal town. Her own daughter — half Turkish and the spitting image of her Turkish grandmother — attends a school that is one-third Black. Maggie's company is hiring, and in my field of Human Resources. She sends us new job announcements every month.

We explore real estate every holiday we go back to visit, warmed by the vision of a kinder life and a more affordable house! Somehow, though, in the final analysis, we're Californians, and feel like we'd be transplants, foreigners, no matter how long we lived there. Stories about "lazy Blacks" at an otherwise pleasant party cements this perception.

But is this just a failure of imagination? Should we move? The question haunts us at every visit. Especially when our kids are warmly embraced by their cousins. Leyla drops everything to play with the kids, and her friends line up to be selected by her to join in. Hasan gives Stephen his bath when he's little, plays soccer with him as he grows, and Uncle Ahmed lets him turn the *kofte* on the barbecue — one with real fire!

There's Something About Mary

STACY

We keep getting reports on 6-year-old Stephen — that he's "wild" and "won't settle down" on the playground. We've done everything the school has told us to do, and nothing has changed. At our wits' end, we are talking to a friend who says, "You've got to meet Mary Wilson. She's African-American, has raised her own six kids and over two hundred foster children. She'll know what to do."

For the love of our son, we put aside our introvert selves and invite Mary over for coffee. We describe Stephen's behavior to her.

She says, "He's acting that way because he's being targeted. You need to spend a whole day at school with him. You'll know what's going on after that."

We take her advice. We learn there is one supervisor for the entire playground. Kids are given balls or Frisbees, and the big kids, including our son, kick and throw as hard as they can. Sometimes the other kids are hit. Seldom witnessed, these incidents are reported by both sides, and the big kids are blamed every time. We start working with other parents to divide the playground into two areas: a kicking and throwing area, and a quieter play space. We take time from work to take turns joining the lone monitor to provide a bit more coverage.

In the course of the playground renewal, we learn that it's not just big Black boys, but big whites ones too that suffer; and it's obvious that the smaller kids getting hit with flying Frisbees and balls suffer. Why does school have to be so difficult? We work on changing the school to be a place more sensitive to all our kids. Many besides ours are feeling isolated and targeted in schools designed in the industrial age to produce robot-like beings that flawlessly follow directions and honor all authority, so they can take their places on a production line of the forties or fifties. Problem is, that world is gone, and these schools aren't preparing today's children for the knowledge economy where originality, innovation, and thinking outside the box will become survival skills.

It's a long and difficult journey to make the schools safe for our son, and while we make a little progress, we are far from successful. Our newfound allies, white parents of other big boys, do not see that our son gets an extra dose, that when the boys are caught doing graffiti on the portable classroom wall, their sons are suspended and ours is expelled.

We go to see Mary many, many times, always coming away wiser and with more energy to keep going. She becomes our adopted Granny. "Granny" confirms what we know, that Black kids have it much harder, and she gives us ideas on how to work around that tough reality, beginning with showing up and seeing what's going on.

Even with my Ph.D. in psychology, I don't hold a candle to this high school graduate when it comes to knowing about kids, schools, family, and community. She heads a strong, proud matriarchal family consisting of herself (the grandma), her two daughters, and their children, all residing under one roof. You can't walk down the street with Mary without someone stopping to say hello and giving her a kiss on the cheek.

From Minority to Majority, Temporarily

STACY

We're in Eleuthera, an island in the Bahamas, on vacation at Club Med. We go to Club Med not because we like it that much, but because it has kids' programs so Barb and I can actually sit on the beach for a little while and read a book. The kids are 6 and 8.

The only Black people we see here are the people who wait on us, who serve the food, give out the towels. The other guests don't even look at these people. It's as if they are invisible. We try to make eye contact, with waiters and waitresses and the man who hands out the towels, but they look suspicious and avoid our eyes.

I go venturing past the doors of Club Med and discover the island and its people. Everyone I meet is Black. I find an art store and fall in love with a beautiful ocean painting on a piece of driftwood. To the surprise and consternation of the shop owner, I ask to meet the artist before buying the painting.

The artist agrees to meet. In fact, she invites us to her home to meet her whole family. It's a busy lived-in home, like our own. The kids are lively and outgoing, and reach out to ours, sharing their toys. We talk about how in the world I am going to ship the painting home. In walks her cousin who happens to work in shipping at the airport. He stands tall and looks me straight in the eye, flashing a beautiful, open smile.

I'm startled. I don't think I've ever met a Black man who has his bearing, his confidence. He's not afraid of me. He doesn't lower his eyes, nor does he try to stare me down. This is his island and his people. He's open because he's safe. I don't remember ever seeing this in the U.S. His look — open, undefended, curious — takes my breath away.

We go to dinner with our new friends. They delight in our kids, enjoying our daughter's stories about what fun things she's been doing, and laughing when our son and theirs crack open coconuts with machetes. At home, our son would not be holding a machete for any reason. He would be perceived as wielding a weapon with intent to kill. The "evil, budding criminal" paradigm would be in full operation.

Another day, on a visit to Nassau, Barb and I are the only white people in the restaurant. Our son and daughter look around, somewhat confused but happy. Stephen exclaims, "Hey, Mom, Matu[4], everyone in here is Black!"

We are honored that our kids include us in that statement, and we wonder if we should move to the Bahamas.

---

[4] "Matu" is Stephen's nickname for me, Mama #2.

The Cage

BARB

Stephen's second-grade year seems to be going really well. He completes the year without once getting sent to the principal's office. We are thrilled, and praise the teacher, an Asian-American man.

Unbeknownst to us, however, the teacher regularly locks Stephen up in a big animal cage in the classroom when he misbehaves. He also calls our son "stupid" and "a baby" in front of the class. Stephen never tells us and no one else knows either, not even the principal. We don't learn the truth until Stephen tells us five years later. At this point, we suddenly understand why since second grade Stephen has shown great anger and mistrust of Asian-American people, except for two Japanese-Americans and one Chinese-American who are among his best friends.

So here is a real dilemma for us. There are some Asian-Americans we know who have physically punished their children, saying it is the way to make sure a child pays attention, learns, and does well in all endeavors. Several have explained that it is part of the culture. We wonder if that was why this teacher treated our son so harshly. One of Barb's friends tells her his father beat him so hard it broke his leg. He says this without resentment, patiently explaining to her that his father loved him enough to discipline and prepare him for the real world. (This guy made straight As throughout college.)

But we don't believe in physical punishment or the belittlement of a child. We finally decide it's one thing if parents choose to enact these kinds of punishments in their own homes — certainly the well-behaved, stellar students coming out of Asian-American homes argue in favor of this method of child-rearing. But it's another matter when these methods are used on our kids, in a public setting.

When Stephen finally tells us this story at age 12, we tell him we're so sorry he was treated like this. We say that no matter what he was doing, the way he was treated was wrong and should not have happened. If we'd known about it, we would have made it stop. Stephen nods, knowing this is true, and says he felt so bad about himself he didn't want to talk about it at the time.

We try to find the teacher. He's moved on to another school district and our district doesn't know where he is.

The Pain Olympics
STACY

We have a dear friend who is African-American and she tells us that when one oppressed group says they are more oppressed than another group, we're into the "Pain Olympics": who hurts more, who has it worse, who deserves more attention.

Her view is that this kind of comparison serves only to pull everyone down and take away from efforts to achieve equality for all. We agree. We've been in gatherings, social events, conferences, etc., where the conversation engaged in this kind of "Pain Olympics."

Our friend reads an early version of this book, and suggests we're into the Pain Olympics. We are very hurt and deeply unsettled. We rewrite the book and rewrite it again. In the end, we suspect we cannot avoid this aspect of our story. We reluctantly believe that we will never move beyond the subtle ways we destroy the spirit of those who are different if we never describe and learn to recognize all the ways we are doing just that. Other African-American friends who read the manuscript adamantly agree with us.

Still, we wish there were some way to put a happy face on our story, or somehow glide over it. Barb constantly brings up the Japanese-Americans who lost everything, herded into labor camps during World War II. Would figure skater Kristi Yamaguchi ever have won an Olympic gold medal if her family had not moved on from the horrors of being interned in a prison camp? How did they do it?

Yet, Japanese-Americans did not forget or even move on until they had described the outrage, advocated for and won at a national level a full apology for this experience. Maybe they, too, were using the dual strategy we've waged: keep the kids' feet to the fire, ensuring they move along and progress, even as the parents take on the system. Barb is constantly asking Asian-American friends for their strategies.

In the end, I wonder what would happen to our identities if we didn't diss one another and we stopped telling negative stories. Could we forge a kind of unity that allows for the differences among us, yet also allows for aligned efforts together?

We are often torn apart by the Powers That Be trying to set us against one another. Let's do the opposite of what is expected. Let's accord one another respect and wish one another peace and well-being.

'You're Just as Prejudiced'

STACY

We're attending the Greek Orthodox baptism of my brother's twin boys. And we have our kids with us, now ages 7 and 9. I'm a nervous wreck. I can't imagine how this is going to go. I'm certain no one really supports our family and they'd all rather we'd just disappear. Even though we've made progress since the memorial service, I expect the worst.

We're in the church and just before the service begins, one of my cousins asks my daughter to come up where the baptism ritual is taking place and help out with the infants. We watch Shawna parade happily around the baptismal font, helping to carry the babies back and forth and dressing them when the baptism is over.

I'm disoriented. How did this happen? This isn't what I expected! I assumed my family would act polite but disapprove of us and find ways to leave us out. Thankfully, Shawna is completely oblivious to my preconceptions and simply takes what she sees to be her rightful place in this mix of her cousins and aunts and uncles.

I stay up all night with my cousins talking and laughing after the ceremony. The next morning another cousin and I are eating breakfast together. I totally love this woman. She and I were very close growing up. I tell her that I miss her. She asks why I haven't I been in touch. She'd love to see me.

"Does that mean all of us?" I ask.

"Of course, why wouldn't it?"

I share with her my fears, my experiences of racism and homophobia in our family.

"It really hurts me that you lump me in with everyone else. You know, you're just as prejudiced as the people you are calling prejudiced. You've never asked me how I felt. You just assumed. Did you know that my two stepsons, who I've raised since they were 7, are gay? They're now 23. I'm a member of PFLAG (Parents and Friends of Lesbians and Gays), and I bet I've been in more gay bars than you have!"

I am stunned. She is right. My own prejudice is blinding me to people who want to be in our lives. It's hard not to assume you'll be rejected when you've been hurt. Prejudging others becomes a defense ... and an excuse.

From that day on, my family and I are in regular contact with this cousin and other family members who accept us. It becomes one of the great joys of my life.

Kumar and Lata Invite Us In

BARB

My dear friend Kumar and his wife, Lata, have invited us into their home and their lives. Lata is an amazing cook and we've had some of the most delicious vegetarian Indian food we've ever tasted.

They have two daughters. Their 11-year-old, Mina, dances traditional Indian dances, and we get to attend dance recitals that are breathtakingly beautiful, followed by receptions with many Indian families. After the first event, Stephen comes to us and asks, very seriously, if 7-year-olds can marry 11-year-olds.

An interesting aspect of getting to know this family is that while Mina is more traditional, like her mother, the younger sister, Sarita, is a rebel. Lata very much wants her daughters to observe traditional Indian customs and religion. Kumar is more laid back. The whole question of assimilation and what it means to assimilate or not has been at the heart of their family.

Being in relationship with this family is teaching us more deeply that tension between cultures is inevitable, and it helps us see how others resolve or at least live more gracefully with these challenging dilemmas. We're also very grateful when people allow us into their lives in a way that shows us who they really are. This is a gift we cherish.

Mogley and Sleep Arrive

STACY

Our son can't sleep through the night. That's been true since he was 2. He's now 8. He wakes up with nightmares. Sometimes he's drenched in sweat. This kid who walks around with macho bravado during the day is terrified at night. Often, he comes into our room to get comfort. It does no good to just tuck him into bed again, because he just wakes up. We put a sleeping bag by our bed so he can crawl in and finally get some sleep and so can we — if we can just get back to sleep!

One morning I wake up with a very clear thought. We need to get a dog for Stephen. And not just any dog. A big dog. A sweet and playful dog. And this dog needs to sleep in Stephen's room. The only time Stephen has been able to stay in his room all night is when he has friends sleep over. That's when he feels comforted, secure, and safe. Especially with his homeboys, Granny Mary Wilson's two grandsons, who are a year older and younger than Stephen. So it's either adopting another boy child or getting a dog. A dog is the clear choice.

I tell Barb my brainstorm. She looks at me like I'm stark raving mad (we already have two cats and a puny goldfish and can barely manage those pets).

"Have you ever *had* a dog?" she asks.

"No."

"Well I have," she declares, "and in a word, they are work! A lot of work! Almost-like-having-another-kid kind of work! They don't even wear diapers — let's start there!"

She is right, I know, but this intuition of mine, this knowing, is strong and deep. I persist and Barb finally agrees to call a friend at work whose sweetheart works at the local pound. We describe the dog we want: at least half Rottweiler (this is what Stephen has decided after doing research on the web), and it must be big, full grown, have a fierce bark (Stephen), be gentle (moms), be fully potty trained (moms), have brown or black coloring (part of our ongoing program to establish positive associations with these colors so maligned in our culture), and be friendly with cats (moms). Barb is relieved since surely there is no dog on earth that fits this profile, but at least she looks like she's giving it a try to find one.

Within a week Barb's friend calls to say his girlfriend has the perfect dog for us. On the way to see "our" dog, we look at all the cute puppies and other dogs in the pound. Then we meet Mogley, part Rottie, part Lab, part shepherd, with beautiful huge brown eyes, and a coat that's golden with shades of black, brown, and white — the color of our family! We all love him. We fill out the paperwork and take him home.

The first night, Barb goes in to tell Stephen it's time to stop playing with the dog and go to sleep. She finds both of them sound asleep: two fuzzy heads on the pillow, the flannel comforter pulled up to both necks, one of them — it's hard to tell which — lightly snoring, and both of them out like lights.

Stephen has slept through just about every night since.

Sure There's Equal Opportunity — as Long as You're Superior

STACY

Hank, our kids' African-American "adopted Dad" and godfather, is the most senior level African-American man at Barb's company, which has more than 100,000 employees. He was the student body president at his Southern white college in the early sixties, and eventually earned a Ph.D. We are having a conversation with him about affirmative action and equal opportunity. He thinks AA/EEO is fine, as long as no person of color — and certainly not Stephen or Shawna — has any illusion about what it really means, which is: If you're a person of color, you have to be superior to have equal opportunity.

Barb points out the total contradiction of having to be superior to be equal. Hank insists — and does so very matter-of-factly. He tells our kids, "It's just the way it is." He wastes no time, no energy in complaints about this absurdity.

Hank says he doesn't really like the focus on diversity. He thinks that focusing on people's differences just makes the problem worse. He'd rather look for what we have in common.

Where's the line between working with things as they are and just giving up? When do you say, "Things might be this way now, but we need to change them for the future"? Barb and I have always focused on diversity. Hank clearly doesn't. Is there something beyond focusing on diversity and not focusing on diversity?

Parade in Calistoga

BARB

We've gotten away for two days for some time alone — the first time in almost two years. We're in a small spa town in Napa Valley. Stacy is shopping while I wait on the sidewalk watching the town's first Cinco de Mayo parade.

I start chatting with the woman next to me, observing, "The parade here is so different from the parade where we live. The theme here is, 'Together we can do it! *Si se puede — juntos!* Let's build a big pool for our town's kids.' At home the theme is, 'Who are the best, brightest, biggest, smartest?' And everybody is competing for the prize. Parents get mad at each other thinking somebody's cheated to beat them or their kids. A week ago a soccer mom screamed at me that our daughter should be removed from the game. 'It's not fair that she's made so many points!' she yelled."

"Yes," says the parade mom, "we used to live in your town. The best thing we ever did was leave and come here. Here it's truly the village that raises the child. If my kid skipped school, by 9 a.m. I'd be hearing from the principal and the police who were out looking for her. There, my kid had been skipping school for three months before a teacher mentioned it in passing in the semester meeting."

"Well," I say, snuggling into the emotional space I enter when I'm on a plane with a friendly and intelligent seatmate, "we're also a two-mom family and our kids are African-American."

Without skipping a beat, the parade mom says, "Our kids are adopted too. Does everyone there look at you like you're crazy for the life you've chosen? With no appreciation for your courage and the strength it takes to live each day?"

That's exactly what it's like. People looking at you like you're crazy or pitiful. No appreciation for what it takes.

What Country Are They From?

BARB

We're at a local event for someone speaking on peace and justice issues. Many folks from our town are there, and we start up conversations with some people we've never met before.

At one point, we're talking with a couple, and when our kids, now 9 and 11, walk by, we introduce them. Both the man and woman smile, and as the kids walk off, he asks, "What country are they from?"

We smile back. I say, "They were born in this country, and their great-greats arrived on these shores before mine did."

Their question is not an uncommon one. Nevertheless, it never ceases to amaze me. What is the assumption behind it? What's the belief or worldview that prompts it? That we wouldn't adopt ordinary or underprivileged Black American kids, just special or exotic foreign ones? Or worse, that Black kids are "foreign" by definition?

Is He Hungry?

BARB

We're in Puerto Vallarta, Mexico, on vacation, shopping in a jewelry store. Our daughter, now 12, and her best friend, and our son, now 9, and two of his best friends are with us. The boys start getting a little squirrelly, especially our son who is having a hard time being still while we shop.

A young Mexican salesman approaches us, and Barb and I tense. We're waiting for "the look," the request to leave the shop.

The young man says in Spanish, "Your son seems disquieted. Is there anything I can do to help? Is he hungry?"

We are stunned by his compassion, his generosity, his openness, and his total lack of fear of our large, agitated boy. We say, yes it's quite possible all the kids are hungry since it has been a while since we've eaten breakfast. The young man smiles and walks away.

Soon, the kids are all eating pizza. The young Mexican salesmen who have given away their lunches to our kids are smiling, laughing. Suddenly, we hear our son's voice broadcast through the store, "Attention, attention, spill on aisle nine." We panic — what is he doing?

But the Mexican men laugh. They've taken our boys in the back room to play with walkie-talkies, and the boys are ecstatic.

We can't stop talking about this incident and its stark contrast with most of our experiences at home. Of course we buy some jewelry! And wonder if we should move to Mexico.

Don't Move to the Music

STACY

We've had several calls from our son's music teacher that he is having behavioral problems in his fourth-grade music class, where the kids are learning to play the recorder and preparing for a concert. I'm surprised that music is a problem for Stephen. As a musician myself, I write, sing and play music, and dance and sing with the kids all the time. We love it.

I attend a class to see what's happening. The teacher has the kids stand in "concert format" to practice the music. She puts on a cool piece of jazz music, which they will be playing to. I watch my Stephen. He starts moving to the music. The teacher yells at him to stop moving, that he needs to stand still!

What? Don't move to the music? Don't move to the very cool rhythms of this music?

After class, I talk to the teacher. I explain that when my son, daughter and I are out riding in the car, we crank up one of the top pop or R &B stations and sing at the top of our lungs, with the kids doing cool dance moves (as best they can in a car). She looks at me rather opaquely, nods, and says she understands. Then she tells me that this is a concert, not a free-for-all jam session where the kids can do anything they want. She emphasizes that she needs to have control to produce a "good" concert.

I try to advocate for the kind of music and concert that would allow the kids' natural energy and rhythms to be incorporated, but the teacher's eyes go blank and she clearly wants to proceed to the next parent waiting to talk with her.

Sometimes I feel just crazy. Am I the only one who thinks "don't move to the music" is an oxymoron?

Discrimination? Believe It

BARB

We're sitting in the office of the school superintendent (again) attempting to solve a problem related to a conflict between Stephen, now 10, and the O'Neil family and their son Patrick.

The school superintendent, the assistant superintendent, and a local police captain are present. As we tell the story about the latest targeting of our son, the superintendent turns to the police captain, who is an African-American, and asks him if he knows of any other incidents like this, or if he has personally experienced discrimination.

Capt. Charles Bailey is a quiet man and hasn't said much up to this point. Now he nods and says, "Yeah, this is a strange little town. The other day I was in uniform serving papers on someone. A woman opened the door and saw me. She said, 'Son, we take deliveries in the back.'"

"I said, 'I'm not a delivery person; I am with the police department.'"

The superintendent looks shocked and says, "I find it difficult to believe that something like that could happen in this town."

Capt. Bailey gives a wry smile. "Believe it."

Disbelief

BARB

I'm watching Stephen in a soccer game and talking with a soccer dad about our sons. He's commenting on my son's size — 5 inches taller than the other 10-year-olds — and I explain that Stephen has been increasingly bigger than his peer group since the age of 2. Now, nearly 10, he is 5-foot-5½-inches tall and wears a size 11 men's shoe — he's the size of an average 14-year-old. On the side of his birth family that Stephen favors, the men regularly reach 6-foot-7-inches. According to our pediatrician, Stephen is growing on that scale.

I also tell my soccer-dad buddy about the recent events with some parents targeting our son, having to go to the superintendent, and hearing the Black police captain tell about being taken for a delivery boy — despite his uniform — and being spoken to as such.

The dad looks at me in surprise, and says, "Oh, that's not *racism*. The woman just thought he was delivering something."

I'm taken aback. "How do *you* define racism?"

"You know, when there are racial epithets, graffiti, like that."

In other words, the overt stuff. I respond by saying that there is also the pernicious, covert kind of racism, the kind that's breaking my little boy's heart. He doesn't get it. We stop talking and sit side by side, unspeaking, for the rest of the game.

I feel so alone and crazy. What do you do when someone tells you that you haven't really experienced what you've experienced?

The Sound of One Hand Clapping

BARB

Our lives have become unmanageable. We believe our family and our son are in danger from the O'Neils, and that both families need additional help at this point in order to work out a plan for living together peaceably in the school and the larger community.

We write Stephen's principal to request mediation with the O'Neil family and a third party to work out a plan that includes how we will coach and support our sons and the consequences for any misbehavior on either side. Whether the third party should come from the district, the police department or the city's Human Relations Commission is up to the principal — we have learned from other parents of African-American children in the district that all these agencies have been known to help in these situations.

We are asking for mediation because our previous meeting as just families failed. We had invited the O'Neils to our home to talk things through. After we heard the boys' stories, we admonished Stephen and imposed consequences that the O'Neils said they thought were fair. We then raised Patrick's taunts as part of the problem and asked about consequences for Patrick. Mark O'Neil jumped up from the couch, turned beet red, came over to my chair while he slapped his fist in his hand. He was furious at the thought that Patrick had anything to do with this situation. We felt afraid of Mark. After regaining some control of himself, he stalked out of the living room, slamming the front door as loud as it can be slammed behind him, whereupon Joann followed.

Mark and Joann are unwilling to look at Patrick's role or to coach him in his behavior toward Stephen. Patrick consistently taunts Stephen, announcing loudly to anyone who will listen that Stephen has two moms, that he's evil, that he's going to jail. This is a form of sexual and racial harassment prohibited by the district.

The soccer season this year began with Patrick's loud, proud greeting to Stephen in front of other kids that he, Patrick, was the reason Stephen was not on the home team, that Stephen is a bad boy and his (Patrick's) parents fixed it so Stephen wasn't on the team with Patrick. I told Patrick to be quiet, but he yelled even louder that it was true, and if I didn't believe it I should go talk to his mom and ask her. (We had requested — as we have successfully done every year except this one — that Stephen be on the home team as he does best with consistency and community. Our request was obviously overridden, with the result that our child was on a team with no kids from his elementary school — a team that his own friends were trying to beat.)

The first soccer game of the season continued with Patrick telling Stephen on the field that he'd grown during the summer and could take him on now. We had already coached Stephen to ignore any further outbursts from Patrick, which Stephen did — something he manages to do about 95% of the time.

We know the O'Neil family is struggling with the fact of our family. Joann has told me that their priest does not agree with our lifestyle, and that Mark has been harassed at work by an African-American man. We also believe in miracles — people change. We both grew up with the very attitudes that the O'Neils are struggling with, and we believe a key is to sit down together.

We believe that the O'Neils are momentarily losing their battle with the demons of racism and homophobia — Joann does not return greetings when we see each other, Patrick's taunting is escalating, and the family has escalated their behavior toward us.

In response to our request, the principal, a great ally, refers us to the police community relations department, which sets up a meeting at the school district office. With great trepidation, we go the meeting. Present are the community relations police officer, the assistant superintendent of schools, Stacy and I. The O'Neils don't show up, nor have they called to say they aren't coming. Clearly they don't want mediation.

How can you have mediation with only one party present? What is the sound of one hand clapping?

Waiting for Godot

STACY

At the meeting, while we're still waiting for the O'Neils — or God or Godot or a miracle — we try to address Stephen's situation at a broader level. After all, I am an ordained minister and a professional diversity trainer, and Barb has a doctorate in psychology. Surely we can raise the level of this discussion and start to look at the roots of the behavior that is so affecting our precious son and every other African-American boy we know.

So we raise the larger issue of racism and other kinds of discrimination in the city as a whole, such as the Neo-Nazi graffiti recently scrawled on the door at the local Jewish Community Center.

With a jovial and intimate tone, the assistant superintendent leans towards us and says, "Now, don't you go worrying about everything that's happening out there. There's a lot of discrimination and that's the way it is. We can only do so much. You just go ahead and take care of your own family."

Inwardly, we groan. What is it that prevents us from looking at larger patterns, both for information and potential solutions? Why do we insist on focusing on things incident-by-incident, as if each incident were an anomaly? Is it denial again? If you only look at problems one at a time, you never see the pattern. You never see the common root of all the problems. You never see the forest, just the trees — hundreds of diseased and stunted trees, each one of them a supposed anomaly.

The school privacy policy, which mandates incident-by-incident and family-by-family solutions, while good on its face, has the pernicious effect of blinding us to the larger patterns and systemic issues, and ultimately prevents a systemic solution.

We remain stubbornly opposed to seeing what several of our friends believe should be obvious: This town is not interested in systemic solutions to racism. It has designed itself with policies and procedures to produce exactly the town we live in.

'You're Evil!'

BARB

In January of 2000, in Stephen's fourth-grade year, I start coming to his elementary school to monitor the 10 a.m. break and noon lunch hour. We believe Stephen is unsafe. The harassment by the O'Neils and their son Patrick has escalated and we are unable to stop it.

One morning when I arrive I learn from Stephen that his school day started with Patrick O'Neil yelling across the campus, "You're evil!" During our past visits to the school campus, both Stacy and I have heard Patrick yell at Stephen that he's bad, he's a bully, and he's trouble. As a result, we have no reason to doubt Stephen today.

At noon, Patrick crosses an entire football field, points at Stephen, shakes his finger, and makes a face until he is sure Stephen sees him, then about-faces and returns across the field to his classroom. (This is a long walk, and since he speaks with no one coming or going, it seems Patrick's sole purpose is to harass Stephen.) I see this whole event occur. Patrick's gesture is mean and deliberately provocative. Stephen has told me about Patrick's pointing and making faces in the past. He says it happens all the time.

At the end of noon recess, Stephen goes to join his friends in a bounce-ball game off the side of the wall outside the classroom. I see Patrick pop his head out of the room and spot Stephen. Patrick's face lights up. Then he looks around, sees me, looks startled, and goes back inside the classroom.

At no time today do I see Patrick with other children or a friend. According to Stephen and his friends, Patrick has no friends. He seems quite focused on harassing Stephen. We have asked Stephen repeatedly to report incidents with Patrick to the principal. He won't. He says he doesn't want to be a tattle-tale, and he'd rather be playing than in the office reporting on Patrick.

The Big Bad Fourth-Grade Bike Chase

STACY

Two days after Barb has exploratory surgery for a suspected highly aggressive uterine cancer (which thankfully the tumor is not), a police officer — a new one, one we haven't met yet — arrives at our house to investigate an allegation by the parents of Patrick O'Neil that Stephen chased their son home from school on his bike. Stephen tells the officer that he and some friends were racing their bikes the two blocks home from school and they passed Patrick, who was biking more slowly. Nothing else happened. No one was chasing anyone and no one was injured. The police officer shakes his head and declares that he has never had such a silly complaint in all his years dealing with elementary school kids.

We are no longer surprised by anything that Patrick or the O'Neils accuse Stephen — or us — of doing. I feel sad when I contrast the way things are to the way it seems they could have been.

At one point, when the boys were in second grade and going at it, Barb invited Joann O'Neil and Patrick for lunch. Joann confided that she disagreed with her priest that our two-mom family was evil, and with her husband, who thought all Blacks were out to get him after a Black co-worker complained about him.

"I'm not like that," she said back then.

Too bad she got so little support for her feelings back then. Too bad that her church is part of the problem, when everything we know about Christianity suggests it should be part of the solution.

Riding Bikes, Shopping = Suspicious Behavior

BARB

Our friend, Yolanda, is over to dinner. Yolanda, an African-American, came to our area from the East, armed with degrees from Harvard and M.I.T., ready to do battle in behalf of kids of color who need support and mentoring.

92

We're talking to her about our experiences with our children and how hard it is to explain what it's like to others, particularly people who cannot imagine there is an issue for kids of color in our area.

Yolanda is debating about leaving this area to go back East again; she's only been here for nine months. She says she imagined it might be different for her out here with respect to racism, but it isn't. We ask what she means. She says she's been stopped twice by the police while riding her bicycle in the nearby, equally affluent town where she lives. Both times, the police wanted to know what she was doing in the neighborhood. She replied that she lives in the neighborhood. She asked them what the problem was. Both times she was told that they had received phone calls from people saying there was "a strange person in the neighborhood."

Yolanda also says she gets followed while shopping. Her most recent example is being followed in a major department store. She says she was in casual clothes, and as she was browsing, noticed a saleswoman following her around. Yolanda stopped and asked the saleswoman if something was the matter. The woman, flustered, said no, she just wanted to know if Yolanda needed any help.

Shawna, now 12, has also told us, "Oh yeah, they always follow us in stores." Stephen, 10, admits he gets stopped as often as two or three times a week by police, who ask where he lives and tell him to go "home," implying that he belongs in the next town over, which is much less affluent and more racially diverse. His reply? "This *is* my home. Do you want to come and meet my parents?"

The truth is, Yolanda, Stacy, and I have a lot more stories like these. But we change the subject, afraid of how quickly we can get caught in negative thinking, start getting bummed out, and spiral down. Defeated by the Pain Olympics. But don't we need to tell each other these things so we don't feel crazy?

I wonder again why these anecdotal accounts are so easily dismissed by people who have never experienced such things themselves. How is it that an "anecdote" is not perceived as real, factual and relevant? And why is it that no matter how many of these anecdotes you recount to those who don't have first-hand knowledge, it's never enough to get a real dialogue going? Is it that the stories themselves indict their victims? Or that those hearing the stories feel indicted?

How can we grow past these stories and past the ignorance and prejudice behind them if the larger community doesn't even acknowledge them as true? But then, have we gotten past slavery yet, or the World War II Japanese-American internment camps, or other events in our nation's history that don't line up with who we think we are today?

Advocacy and Allies

STACY

> If you have come to help me, you are wasting
> your time. But if you have come because your
> liberation is bound up with mine, then let us work
> together.
> — *Lila Watson, an Australian Aboriginal woman*

Allies are the best. Especially when they are the ones
we least expect. And especially when, as Lila Watson's
quotation suggests, their advocacy and support come
from healthy self-interest, not from pity or sympathy. True
allies know that for their own freedom, others must be
free.

Mike was the principal of our first elementary school.
He understands prejudice and confronts it head-on when
he sees it. He believes us when we raise concerns about
our daughter and son, especially when those concerns
involve how they are being negatively treated as Black
kids. Mike is willing to take the heat for advocating in our
kids' behalf. He does this for any kid who needs a voice.

Some parents criticize him, saying he is "lowering
academic standards" in the school by not removing
"troublemakers" — code for Black and Latino kids coming
from outside our town to the school. And this is an
alternative school!

Joe Mason, the principal of our second elementary
school, is a young white male. He taught in the Bahamas
for several years where he was the only white person
around. He has had the visceral experience of being the
"other," and so is conscious of issues around inclusion and
exclusion. He sometimes gets overridden by higher-ups

when he advocates for our kids (especially our son), but he never stops trying.

In our opinion, there is nothing more powerful when it comes to advocacy than having people who are privileged advocate for those who are not, such as when white people speak up for people of color, when heterosexual people speak up for gay, lesbian, bisexual and transgender people, when men speak up for women, and when people who are fully-abled speak up for those who are physically challenged.

Then there are our longtime allies, people who have become part of our family. We've written about the angel that Gina has been in our lives. We also have an African-American family, Granny Mary Wilson and her entire extended family. They're a critical part of who we are. Theirs is a strong, proud matriarchal family: Granny, her two daughters, Lila and Tish, and the grandchildren, all under one roof. Granny is the one who first named what was happening to Stephen ("That baby's being targeted"). Lila has run cool, calm interference for us in incredibly complex situations with our kids, and Tish has patiently and deftly put extensions and braids into Shawna's hair. Grandsons Lionel and Jason are Stephen's "homies" and often hang out with us. These are deep visceral connections. We feel so lucky, so privileged to have been let in, to see and be a part of a world that we knew nothing about before we had our kids.

All of these allies and angels have been, and continue to be, a source of the deepest love and support.

You're at War With Your Black and Brown People

BARB

We're having our friend Ijeoma to dinner. Ijeoma is an activist from Nigeria. Both her parents were also activists in Nigeria and are now dead, having been assassinated. We share with her our experiences of racism and homophobia where we are living.

She doesn't look surprised or shocked. She simply says, "You're at war with your Black and brown people in this country. All the Africans who come here know it, can see it, and feel it. Only the white people who live here don't see it or name it."

"War" is strong language and not a metaphor that easily comes from Ijeoma, who's been in a war and lost her parents to it. But in our experience "war" feels right, and we ask Ijeoma to say more. She says that after her parents were killed, she brought two of her brothers to the U.S. and put them in the very best schools. After several years, Ijeoma asked her brothers what their dreams were of the future. One brother said he hoped to graduate high school without being arrested. The other said he really liked video games and wanted to grow up so he could play them full-time.

Ijeoma was alarmed. While it was clear to her that if she sent her brothers back to Nigeria, their lives could be in danger, it was better than leaving them here where their minds and hearts were shutting down and their spirits dying a slow death.

So she sent them back to Nigeria. Now, a year later, one of her brothers dreams of becoming the next president, the other plans to be a doctor.

We wonder, should we move to Nigeria? Ijeoma thinks we should. We read about African-American movie stars and their homes in other countries where they are raising their kids. One talks about leaving this country where his kids are under siege. Bill Cosby's beautiful son is killed on the freeway while he awaits AAA for a car repair. We wonder, *When did the Jews who escaped the Holocaust know it was time to leave? How do we discover that subtle line that, once crossed, means there's no future for you, that it's time to flee for your lives? Have we already crossed that line in America?*

We arrange for "safe houses" with friends in Switzerland and in Canada, and ensure all four of our passports are up to date.

One Hand ... Flapping

BARB

We write the PTA chair and our principal, letting them know of the failed mediation with the O'Neils, and that we still need help at the local, school level.

By this point there are a lot of rumors and much gossip circulating among parents at the elementary school about our family and our son. We are very concerned at the way stories are growing and being embellished — based on incidents that have already been handled and put to rest by the principal, or that never happened in the first place.

People are calling us to tell us which side they are on, or to find out more from us before they decide which side they are on. What is of concern here is that there are "sides" developing and this whole situation is escalating. We wonder if there is anything that the PTA chair and the principal can do with the parent community.

For the record, we lay out for the rumors and facts.

Rumor (started by a parent, Marsha Dimone): Two years ago at the Haunted House, Stephen poked his fingers in the eyes of other children. Marsha says she told him to stop, let him back in only when he promised to stop, and then caught him at it again.

Fact: Marsha Dimone didn't tell us about this at the time, nor did she report it to anyone else. We have no way of knowing if this is true. We suspect it is not.

Rumor: This fall, Stephen put a child in a headlock during a football game and the child passed out. Marsha Dimone's son told her about this and she went to several families to inform them of the Haunted House incident and that Stephen is dangerous, brutal and violent. Then she stormed into our house and started yelling at Stephen — which is how we learned about the alleged Haunted House incident — and told us how she'd been warning other families about our son and his parents. At that time she did not say anything to us about a child having passed out.

Fact: Some of the boys were playing touch football on the way home. It turned into tackle football. Stephen tried a move he'd seen on TV on another child and it hurt. The kids went home and nothing more occurred. No one passed out. We spoke to the family of the child in question and let them know Stephen was very inappropriate, can no longer watch the TV program in question, and had lost his bike privileges as a consequence. They were glad we called, and said that they hadn't thought there was any problem until Marsha Dimone came in with her stories. Their kid had come home and said he'd been in a tackle football game and had been tackled. The school principal investigated the football incident, since it occurred on the way home from school, and handled it with all the boys in question.

Rumor: We have heard from one family that Marsha Dimone is telling people there are "lots of incidents" with Stephen, "lots and lots of parents" who have problems with our family, and many people who won't let their kids play with Stephen.

Fact: We know nothing about these incidents, or the parents, or the kids. We had a birthday party recently for Stephen and invited 40 kids, and 40 kids came. Most of their parents came, too, and we had many good conversations.

Another Fact: Because teachers reported that Stephen was having a tough year and being sent out of the classroom to sit alone for hours on end for being disruptive, it was recommended that he get 20 hours of observation by the district to see what kinds of situation were difficult for him. The behaviorist hired by the district came out and observed Stephen in every school setting — classroom, recess, lunch, etc. She called us before she wrote her report because she was baffled: *She had found nothing to distinguish Stephen's behavior from that of any other 10-year-old boy.*

We ask for help to keep our family and child safe. We believe the atmosphere arising around the Knight Initiative[5] — including demonstrations in front of churches in town — is part of the picture at the moment. Needless to say, we are not asking anyone to approve our lifestyle, only to let us live in peace.

The PTA chair and the principal do not formally respond. However, our letter seems to have helped. We also learn through other parents concerned for us that, in the words of one of them, "the vigilante committee" targeting our family all belong to the same church. This denomination was one of the two biggest funders of the Knight Initiative — the other big funder was another denomination.

---

[5] The Knight Initiative was California Proposition 22 on the 2000 ballot. It stated, "Only marriage between a man and a woman is valid or recognized in California." It was passed on March 7, 2000 with 61% approval, which constituted a majority of 23%.

A Solution That's No Solution
STACY

In a terrified moment, we go to see a lawyer. We are advised that there is not much we can do legally at this point to stop the vigilantes. We can file a restraining order against Marsha Dimone and the O'Neils, and/or we can file a lawsuit for defamation. This isn't going to stop their behavior. It will cost a lot of money and bring unwanted publicity to our family and, most of all, to our kids.

We decide to keep plugging away, keep trying to get people to sit down and talk with us, and keep praying our son will survive the harassment without ending up an angry and bitter boy and, soon, an angry and bitter young man.

Jailed
BARB

Our son is in the fifth grade and is spending most of his time in the principal's office because the teacher is afraid of him and cannot deal with his being in her classroom. This is her first year teaching. She has 34 kids and no aide. She apologizes profusely every time we see her and assures us that Stephen is not the only one living in the principal's office. We ask her if there is anything we can do to help, but she just throws up her hands.

One night I ask Stephen how school is going, and he says, "I feel like I'm in jail."

Gay Marriage

BARB

It's February 2000. The beautiful house down the street, always clean and cheerful looking, with reindeer in the yard at Christmas and a Valentine flag flying on February 14th, now sports a new decoration: a big "Save Marriage" sign, a symbol and affirmation of the latest effort at making everything harder for families like ours.

Suddenly this house looks ominous to me, the older couple who putter in their yard, sinister. I find myself driving the longer way home so that I don't have to pass this full-of-dread spot, which is in my neighbor's yard, on my street, in my space.

I wonder if they know about us living down the street. Would they care if they knew the thousands of dollars we've spent, and the additional thousands of dollars of state resources, that have gone into paperwork and social workers so our children can have the same legal protections as the kids in the neighborhood with straight — and thus legally married — parents? Do they have any idea what it's like to rush a child to the emergency room with a broken arm, as Stacy has, and spend an additional hour with our agonized daughter waiting to see the doctor while the staff checks that she's a "real" mother? Somehow I don't feel like going up to this house and introducing myself to see if we can have a conversation. Just the thought of it is so exhausting it makes me want to sleep for a year.

Although we contribute to equal rights financially and have registered as domestic partners with the state and with my company, we haven't marched or waved banners for gay marriage. We're too tied up with schools, homework, PTA, soccer and dance, not to mention demanding more-than-full-time jobs.

If we're just too tired, we're also just too angry. Adoptive parents have to pay thousands or tens of thousands of dollars to spring kids out of foster care and orphanages, and gay parents pay additional thousands on top of that to get our children less than full legal protection. The hypocrisy of the pious trying to "protect" families while their actions work to destroy our own is more than we can take on as a cause right now. Our neighbors are just people we'll do better to stay clear of.

Watching Each Other's Backs

STACY

Since they were very young, Shawna and Stephen have been very protective of each other. It's okay if they call each other names, but watch out if anyone else does! One afternoon as I am picking up Stephen, 10, from elementary school, Shawna, who's 12 now, comes rushing to my car. She has walked over to Stephen's school from her middle school next door and seen something that made her very angry.

As I roll my window down, Shawna yells, "They're blaming Stephen and it wasn't his fault! I saw the whole thing!" Someone had pushed a kid hard and he fell to the ground. The supervising adult, who didn't actually witness the event (he had his back to the kids), turned around, saw Stephen, and immediately assumed he was the one who did the pushing.

Shawna, still outraged, walks with me to the principal's office where she proceeds to tell the principal about what she saw. Because she witnessed the event, and is known as a kid who does not lie, the principal believes her and goes outside to set the record straight with the supervising adult.

Shawna and Stephen continue to grow closer. We know that each supports the other, and that we probably have no idea of all the ways they have helped one another get out of tough spots. That's one of the great things about having a sibling.

Love me, love my brother. Love me, love my sister.

Finally, Two Legal Moms

STACY

It's 2000. Our lawyer advises that right now — at least for a brief window in time, with the current judge who sits on these cases, and until it's possibly overturned by the "save the family" coalitions — I can apply to co-adopt our kids, even though I'm "same sex."

We're so tired. Do we really have to go through this process? We know we do. Everything from our wills to hospital emergencies will be better for our kids if I'm also their legal parent. With a heavy heart, I begin the process. Once again, there's a ton of paperwork, two intrusive visits from social workers into our home, and interviews by the worker with each of the kids, separately, to ensure they know I will become their legal parent. Of course, first we have to explain that so far I am *not* a "real" parent, which (though they both already know this) disturbs them when we bring it up.

Finally, we all head down to the judge's chambers, and I'm granted co-adoption parental status. We celebrate with a big meal at the Vietnamese restaurant around the corner from the courthouse!

How Dare You?

STACY

I'm on a panel at an elementary school. There are six of us talking with the fifth-grade student body on issues of diversity and tolerance. I've done this kind of thing frequently, since my work has been in the field of diversity, and I have a lot of interest in what happens in the schools. When it's my turn to speak, I talk first about being a two-mom family with two adopted African-American children. The rest of the time I spend discussing what that means in terms of diversity and living in our community. I focus on the issue of race.

The next day I get a call from Sandra, an African-American woman and the friend who had invited me to sit on the panel. She says that one of the dads from the elementary school had called her, furiously demanding to know how she dared bring a gay person onto the panel "in front of all the children."

Sandra, who says she often simply cuts this kind of conversation off, decides to engage this man and explain the why of it. She tells him that issues of diversity and tolerance include sexual orientation and families who have two moms, two dads, and other parental configurations. She also says that it is important for kids to hear gay and lesbian people because there are undoubtedly kids in the audience who could be wondering about their sexuality and struggling with it. She adds that gay kids have the highest suicide rate, related to the fact that they can't even discuss their sexuality, or if they do, get a reaction like his.

I deeply appreciate Sandra's advocacy. It is courageous and she really puts herself on the line.

The father goes to the principal to complain. The principal, however, supports Sandra, even though she (the principal) is in a difficult position as someone who needs to be mindful of the concerns of the parents of kids at her school. However, the principal was present at the panel presentation, heard me, and later came up to me to say she really appreciated that I had participated. Another brave act, another ally.

As it turns out, the father who complained — and continues to complain for weeks after the event — wasn't in the audience. He hadn't heard me or any of the other panelists. He refuses my offer to meet, extended on my behalf by both the principal and Sandra.

This whole incident reminds me of my years in the church in one of the many Christian denominations struggling to afford their members the rights and respect long since granted by many corporations. Back then, my fellow female minister who accused me of theological incompetence never once called me to talk, nor would she agree to sit down in my presence with others when I and others invited her to do so. I never met her and saw her only briefly in the audience on the day of my "trial," which she had catalyzed.

Research has demonstrated that demonizing is the first step in the dehumanization process required to kill another person. It seems to me that the first step in demonizing is the refusal to talk to someone whose beliefs or values are different.

What's Hair Got to Do With It, Part 2
STACY

Shawna's turning 13 and has just had her hair permed and styled at her request. The hair stylist tells her not to wash her hair or it will frizz up and she'll lose the style. Shawna covers her hair during her shower, but her hair frizzes anyway.

Shawna is hysterical. She doesn't want to go to her own birthday party, which is at a skating rink with 50 kids who are already at the rink. We're frantic. Carrie, Shawna's best friend, arrives at our front door. We tell Carrie what's going on and ask if she could please talk to Shawna.

The next thing we know, Shawna comes out of her room, smiling and ready for her party.

"What did you say to her?" we whisper to Carrie.

Carrie smiles. "I just told her the truth. I said her hair looks absolutely beautiful and I wish my hair would look like that."

Hair, hair, hair. As Shawna gets older, she wants desperately to look like the other African-American girls. Now she regularly has her hair permed, straightened, and braided, with extensions put in. Her scalp gets burned by the lye, bruised by the pulling, and hurts all night after a treatment. The hairstylist says, "Cold towels on the head, and two Advil for the first two nights."

Why can't our daughter wear her hair in its natural state? What is so fundamentally unacceptable that she and other Black girls and women feel they have to change something so basic about themselves (the operative words being "have to" rather than "choose to")? What are the spoken and unspoken messages they receive about themselves, about who they are? And what is the cost to them of internalizing those messages from such a young age?

To us the hair thing has become a symbol of something larger; exactly what, we don't know, but it's troubling. A message of some kind that Black women can't be stunning without going to these lengths, going through this pain, the long hours, the hundreds and eventually thousands of dollars. We don't want to collude with it, but we don't want our daughter ostracized for not colluding either.

Karen's Perfect Picture

BARB

Our daughter's good friend, Karen, who is white, is a wonderful artist. She gives our daughter a portrait she's done in acrylics on a long silk scarf. It's of Shawna and it's beautiful, sensitive, the very dark skin tone exactly perfect, the high cheekbones, long and slender body, long thin feet.

It's very clear this white girl really "sees" our daughter. How is this possible? Neither of us could have "seen" a Black friend at her age. In fact, at that age we had no Black friends even to imperfectly see. Things are changing; things are getting better. We need to step back and realize this, again and again. It would be a terrific daily mantra if only we could remember to chant. We are so grateful to this miracle of a little artist who can see so clearly. And even more grateful that our daughter has her for a friend.

Sit on Your Own Side of the Street

BARB

One of our son's best friends, Gary, is sitting on the curb opposite his house on the street where he lives in our town. The police arrive and ask him why he is sitting on the curb. Gary, who is 11, says, "I live here. That's my house," he adds, pointing across the street. He asks the police what the problem is.

The police tell him a neighbor (an older white woman) called to complain that this "Black kid" was sitting on the curb in front of her house. The police tell Gary that he needs to get up and go sit on his own side of the street.

Gary tells us this story and we look at each other, shaking our heads. You would think by now we'd be used to this kind of harassment. We're not.

Good Times

STACY

It's 5 o'clock on a Wednesday afternoon. This marks the end of the school week because school is closed Thursday and Friday for staff development days.

Barb is still at work, and I'm at my desk at home finishing up a few things. The door bursts open. In walk five 13-year-old girls, led by our daughter. The air becomes electric with their chatter. Backpacks fly through the air, the refrigerator door opens and food gets stuffed into mouths. A CD is soon blaring. I greet the girls amid the cacophony, ask how they are, how their days went, and am met with "Hi" and "Fine."

The door blows open again and in walks our son, now 11, with his three best friends.

One of the boys is African-American and practically lives at our house. He and our son are like brothers. More backpacks fly around, more food is stuffed into mouths, and more ritual greetings ensue.

Quasi-insults fly between the boys and girls. This is the current manifestation of hormones, and seems to be the preteen/early teen version of flirting. I remind them to be respectful, but can't help smiling to myself ... some of their comments are pretty funny. The boys don't like the CD the girls are playing, so they change CDs and soon are singing and moving to a rap song (all for the benefit of the girls). My son says, "Now there's some *good* Black music." One of the girls says, "Whatever ..." and all the girls flounce off, slamming our daughter's bedroom door behind them.

The girls find a movie they want to watch while they take out my daughter's braids. It's time for a new do, the old braids have to go, and hair is the main event for the rest of the afternoon and evening.

I walk into the family room and what I see in front of me touches me, thrills me, and takes my breath away. Can this really be our lives? Our daughter is sitting on the couch and her friends have completely surrounded her, their white hands holding the end of combs which are furiously moving through her dark hair as the extensions fall to the ground. Chips, dip, hair, and soft drinks are everywhere, and as the girls work and munch, they comment on the movie they're watching. Our daughter sits like a queen surrounded by her attendants.

In the meantime, our son and his three friends are in the backyard pool. They're diving, flipping, running, shouting. I remind them not to hold another's head down, not to dive from the shallow end, never to push, and they keep it together for about two minutes until I have to remind them again. They periodically come dripping into the house, no towels, leaving all the screen doors open. They're ravenous after a couple of hours so we order huge pizzas, which are devoured in seconds.

Our friend Yolanda comes over. She's now commuting cross-country between Washington, D.C., where she mentors kids of color, and our area, where she's the principal of a high school she started. We sit, drink tea, and catch up, our conversation interrupted frequently by the sounds and fury of the nine kids with their agendas, questions and swirling presences.

Yolanda looks at me and says, "Is it like this often here?"

I laugh and say, "Yeah, we run a community center here. Only thing missing are the donations. It ain't cheap!"

At one point, two of our daughter's friends have taken a break and are heading back to her room. I introduce them to Yolanda.

She asks the girls, "Why do you like to be over here?"

One girl answers, "It's peaceful."

The other says, "I feel like I'm listened to."

The answers surprise me. *Peaceful? Is she serious?* I think adults who visit us must leave taking a deep breath and feeling grateful that they get to go home to "peaceful." And "listened to"? By whom? Our daughter? Us? I make a note that I'd like to ask this kid more about what she means, because now I'm really curious.

Yolanda looks at me and says, "You've created something really wonderful here. That must feel good."

"I do love teens. Always have. And I guess I'd rather they're here than a place where I don't know what they're doing. And I suppose it's pretty cool that they like to be here ... we must be doing something right. Even though I feel I can't breathe sometimes, or like I want to run out the door screaming, or just hide, the truth is, I adore these kids. All of them. I like how they think, how they talk, their questions. I like to listen to music with them and rock out in the car. I like that they are still malleable and can be influenced in good ways."

There is real truth in the saying that kids keep you young. I just wish my 53-year-old body didn't tire so easily or so often. My mom has said to me, "Honey, that's why women should have kids young. They have the energy." Yes, but emotional, psychological, and spiritual stamina are also quite helpful. And that, along with some sprinkling of wisdom, is what we chose over youth for this amazing task of raising children.

My daughter and her four friends look up at me hopefully. Shawna asks if they can all spend the night.

"No," I say. "But one or two can stay."

"But Mom, we made a pact that if one of us is invited we *all* have to be invited or no one stays," Shawna protests.

"Really? That's an interesting pact. Did you think of asking us parents before you decided this?"

"Uh ... no. But, I need all of them so my hair can be finished, otherwise I won't be ready for my other hair appointment tomorrow."

Shawna snags me on this one. It's the hair thing again. I, too, really want her hair finished. "Okay, but this is not a commitment that all five of you can always spend the night together over here. Understood?"

They all five nod. I can almost hear their thoughts: *blah, blah, blah.*

Stephen, overhearing this last piece of so-called negotiation, comes bounding in to ask if his best bud can spend the night too.

I bow to the inevitable. "Yes, if his mom says it's okay."

Yolanda, who has been witnessing all this, starts laughing.

I know the next day I will turn into a taxi driver taking kids home, at least some of the kids. I wonder, *Where can you buy one of those yellow taxi signs. I need to put one on top of my car.*

Cable TV: Lesbian Mom in Suburbia

STACY

There is a wonderful husband and wife in the Unitarian church that Barb has joined and which I sometimes attend with her. This couple, separately, are powerful, vocal advocates for the lesbian, gay, bisexual, and transgender (LGBT) community. Bill and Helen put themselves on the line often, speaking out within their church, supporting the visibility of the LGBT community in all aspects of church life. They have sponsored legislation for LGBT rights, chaired the same-sex marriage movement in our region, and done more, a lot more. They are wonderful people, wonderful allies.

Bill comes up to me in church and says, "I work with the local cable TV network and was wondering if you would be willing to be interviewed about being a lesbian mom in suburbia. It's part of the PFLAG (Parents and Friends of Lesbians and Gays) series." A week later I am sitting in a TV studio in front of a camera being interviewed by Bill.

There are about 20 people looking on and though I can't see much of them given the lights, I feel bathed in love and gratitude. I don't always feel that way when I'm talking about my experiences, but I sure do in this situation.

Though I'm introverted, I've also learned how to be comfortable in public speaking arenas, and actually enjoy that part of my work. I've had to work hard to cultivate it. I've always loved interacting with others in a learning, exploratory, dialogic mode. I've seen amazing things happen in these settings, and feel grateful to be a part of these kinds of opportunities.

I get lots of calls and emails after the airing of this segment, which lead to even more dialogue, including some controversy. Some viewers feel there should be a warning before this cable program that it's not appropriate for children, given that it's a gay mom speaking. Bill and Helen take on the conversation, welcoming the fact that people agree to talk. Like me, they don't mind controversy, as long as it remains a respectful interchange.

Bill and Helen are an inspiring example of people of privilege (in this case heterosexual privilege) creating space for those who don't have their advantage.

The Change

BARB

Sometime during our daughter's 13th year, she becomes virtually unrecognizable from the kid she was in grammar school. We witness moodiness, sulkiness, defiance, irritation, and gleeful "ups," driven mostly by hormones. We wonder, "Who is this child and what happened to our daughter?"

This is the lament of many parents of teenage girls, as we learn again and again in talking with other parents. We also remember our own teen years, sneaking around, smiling to the faces of our parents even as we "borrow" money we never ask for and lie about where we're going.

But kids today don't date like we used to. They don't bring boys home to meet the parents. They often gather in packs. Parents may never meet the boys their daughters are seeing. Girls chat on the Internet with God- knows-who. They don't realize the danger they could be facing: anonymous men posing as teens, or worse, men who don't even bother to hide that they're 10, 20, 40 years older than the girl.

Sex and drugs begin early. Who knows how early? What about AIDS? Or STDs like herpes, chlamydia, genital warts, gonorrhea?

"Oh, Mom," our daughter, says. "I'm not having sex. Stop tripping."

All her friends are telling their parents the same thing. They all smile and act like everything's fine. We want to believe it. Then the other shoe drops. One of the girls is pregnant, another has run away and is found living with a man in a very dangerous neighborhood nearby.

"Going to the mall" is revealed as the lie that covers a multitude of dangers. We issue consequences and share information endlessly with other parents as each of us learns a piece of the picture. This seems to keep Shawna relatively safe for the next year or so.

Our stress is going through the roof. We're not sleeping well. Sometime in this period I think, *I'm either going to have a nervous breakdown or a cigarette!* I choose the cigarette and soon am smoking a pack a day — a bad habit I developed during the dissertation years and dropped before we had kids. Bad as it is, and it is bad, it truly feels like the alternative to a complete breakdown, which I am convinced we cannot afford on any level.

'We're Not Safe'

STACY

Another night meeting, for middle-school-age kids, at the community center. The topic is, Do kids of color feel safe in school? Like many of their peers, Shawna and Stephen have refused to go, saying the whole thing is "hokey" and won't change anything anyway.

Slowly, tentatively, the kids who have come start opening up and talking about their experiences. The overall answer they give is no, we don't feel safe. Sometimes the reason is that they get blamed for things they didn't do. Sometimes it's that teachers won't call on them when they have their hands raised.

I share some of the experiences Shawna and Stephen have had. Some of the adults nod knowingly at what I say; others look at me suspiciously.

I think it's important to show up at these kinds of events, even though it may feel like a waste of time. I find myself humming a Holly Near/Meg Christian song[6] that goes:

> *Can we be like drops of water falling on the stone*
> *Splashing, breaking, dispersing in air*
> *Weaker than the stone by far, but be aware*
> *That as time goes by, the rock will wear away.*

Much of the time we simply have to wake up, suit up, show up and have faith that we're making a difference.

---

[6] "The Rock Will Wear Away," © 1977 by Hereford Music/Thumbelina Music (ASCAP). All rights reserved.

Turn Down the Volume

STACY

Tina, a friend of Shawna's and the granddaughter of our wonderful Granny, is in high school. Her mother, Tish, tells us that she has received several calls from the school counselors saying that Tina needs to get a grip on her attitude.

Tish asks what they mean by "attitude."

The counselors say that in this case, "attitude" means Tina speaking her mind and using a tone of voice that is "too loud."

Tish responds by saying that she has taught Tina to speak her mind, and that in the instance the counselor is citing, Tina was doing so about the fact that she was feeling singled out. Tish adds that she thinks "loud" is probably a matter of opinion. She points out that in Black culture, voices are often louder. It's part of the Black spirit, community, and life.

Two weeks later, five girls, including Tina, are suspended from high school for "being too loud and rebellious." All five are African-American. The school sees no connection between the suspension and racism.

Who defines "too loud"? And what is it about "loud" that is so unacceptable? In the Greek community where I grew up, loud is normal. Lots of volume, lots of food, multiple TVs and radios blaring, dancing and eating going on around the clock. It's exciting. It pulses. It's rich with emotion and expression of emotion. By everyone. We often find this kind of experience when we hang with African-American and Latino families. We love it!

Unprecedented Recognition

BARB

The employee magazine published by the Fortune 100 company where I've worked for 17 years writes a very complimentary article about my work. With it, they run a big photo of our family: two white moms and two Black teenagers (both of whom are taller than we are). We are delighted and somewhat amazed. This magazine goes to company employees all over the world, including nations where homosexuality is still illegal. There is some backlash, but there is also a wonderful feeling of acceptance.

The editor calls me after publication to let me know that the article elicits more employee comments than any other story they've ever run, and he wants to let me know he'd like to run a few of the comments, spanning the gamut. Would it be OK? I agree. The comments range from "I so admire Barb and her courage," to "It's very sad to think this company has fallen so far as to feature this lifestyle in its company newspaper. Please cancel my subscription."

I am happy about the good stuff and not surprised by the bad. I wrote the first feminist newspaper column in the country in the early seventies. The first fan letter I received was a voodoo doll with pins in the breasts and vagina. The last, two years later, was from a convicted rapist writing from prison, saying he had me surrounded, detailing what he planned to do to me. He sent his letter to my new office address — which wasn't to be assigned for another two weeks. One of the many great things about that experience is that it set a new standard for "bad." This "bad" isn't even close. And as before, the good far outweighs the bad.

He'll Have to Be a Man at 11

STACY

We're sitting in our living room with a woman police officer who's an African-American friend of a friend. We're talking about our son and the fact that he is accumulating police reports. We know this can be deadly for a large African-American boy.

The police officer listens quietly to our concerns for a while, then says, "I'm not going to pull any punches here. I'm going to tell it the way I see it."

"Fine. That's okay by us. The truth is better than any sugarcoating at this point."

The officer says, "Your son needs to understand that life will not treat him fairly. It will be that way until he dies." She pauses to take a deep breath. "I struggled all the way over here about how to tell you that he needs to be a man and act like a man at 11 years old. Otherwise, the potential consequences for him are very scary."

We listen to her, knowing in our hearts that she's telling the truth and she knows this truth personally. We invite Stephen into the conversation and she tells him what she's told us.

"Do you understand what I'm saying?" she asks.

Stephen nods.

"You have to learn to blow off the people who hurt you. Pretend they don't exist and don't give them any energy. I know this is a very hard message, but if you get it, you can have a good life."

Our son bows his head and looks at the floor.

As the officer heads for the door, there's one remaining question.

"How does an 11-year-old be a man? Especially when he loves being 11 and *is* 11?" We ask that out loud of the officer and of ourselves. It's a rhetorical question really.

What does it mean that a child must sacrifice his childhood in order to survive?

She smiles ruefully and says, "That's just the way it is." We know this already, but it hurts to hear it said so bluntly. Even so, it is strangely comforting to hear it out loud.

How Do I Get Up?

STACY

I'm lying in bed, feeling an overwhelming depression and sadness. I'm thick with inertia. It's been about a week since we talked with the policewoman, then heard the latest cruel rumor circulating about Stephen — that he's in jail. I get ready to track this one down, try yet some other way to stop this crap, and then, I just can't get up.

What kind of a parent am I if I can't even protect my son from this kind of thing? It's like having your heart live outside your body and having no way to protect it. I think, *If he ends up in prison, they better have a cell right next to his for me because there's no way in hell I'll let him go through that alone.*

It becomes hard to move. I wonder how to get through another day. I wonder even if I can. I think about all the parents of color with their children and wonder how they get through their days. Thinking of their courage and tenacity, I manage to swing my legs over the side of the bed and get started with whatever might be next.

I notice that over the next several weeks I have difficulty leaving the house. I don't really want to talk to anyone. Everyone appears like a potential enemy, someone who'll turn us in. The world shrinks and quickly becomes divided into us and them. But it doesn't feel like there is much "us."

I know we have to continue to find allies, build community, and that we have to do it soon. Even though we are very, very tired and I am afraid to leave the house.

Whatever made us think we could raise these kids? What have we done?

Harry Potter?

BARB

Teachers have been telling us for years that our son can't read, that he's behind and it will be difficult for him to catch up. We work with him, listening while he reads aloud.

In the summer of Stephen's 11th year, my friend Nancy, who's always looking out for us, gives us a book called *Yo, Little Brother!* written by two African-American men and addressed to African-American boys. The focus of the book is helping young Black boys to survive in America. One of the first chapters raises the all-important question, "How to walk into a store," and one of the last begins, "Who do you think they're building all those prisons for anyway?"

Our son suddenly starts reading out loud with no difficulty whatsoever. Stephen, who just finished fifth grade, is interested, asks questions, and refers to the back of the book to see which man is telling which story. He's sitting in a bathtub, bubbles everywhere, his little head poking up over the bubbles, and reading away.

I ask Stephen, "How are you reading a book for high-school kids when your teachers say you can't read at a fourth-grade level?" He says, "Mom, you know what they give me to read there? Harry Potter! What has that got to do with me?"

We order Shaquille O'Neal's autobiography, and Ben Carson's, and Colin Powell's.[7] There's no more problem with Stephen's reading per se, just with assigned reading that has nothing to do with his life — which is pretty much all of the assigned reading.

The Victim Got the Same Punishment
STACY

We're talking with the man who will be Stephen's teacher when he starts sixth grade shortly at our local public middle school. He's a young white man who is a

---

[7] *Shaq Attaq!* by Shaquille O'Neal (Hyperion, 1993); *The Big Picture* by Ben Carson (Zondervan, 2000), about a frustrated inner-city kid who grows up to be director of pediatric neurosurgery at Johns Hopkins; *My American Journey* by Colin Powell (Random House, 1995).

lawyer as well as a teacher. We're weighing our words carefully, trying to express our concern about Stephen's history in school, his academic struggles, and the issues of overt and covert racism. We don't want to sound like rabid moms — especially rabid lesbian moms.

The teacher doesn't miss a beat. He says, "Yeah, we think of this town as so liberal and cool. Last week, there was a fight between two boys, one white and one Black. The white kid pulled a knife on the Black kid. The Black kid was defending himself and the two fought. The outcome was that *both* boys were suspended. They got equal consequences." He frowns. "Do you think if it had been the Black kid who pulled the knife that the white kid would have been suspended? And the Black kid would be back in school a few days later?"

We leave the meeting feeling like our son could have a very good first year in middle school.

A Molehill Becomes a Mountain (Range)

BARB

Stephen is 11, sitting on the playground with two girls, Samantha and April, also 11. He and Samantha start spitting food at each other, laughing and joking. Samantha leaves to wash her face, and Stephen and April finish her lunch. Samantha comes back, laughs, and calls her mom to ask for another sandwich. So far, we have an incident the size of a molehill, one that neither Stephen nor the principal mention to us.

The molehill grows. Samantha's mom, Mrs. Osman, storms out to the playground to deliver the sandwich, sees Stephen and feels "pure rage" (as she tells us later), and starts screaming at him to leave her daughter alone. Samantha and Stephen are totally embarrassed. Samantha's mom asks the principal to call the police. He refuses and instead tells her that it was inappropriate and against policy for her to confront a child like this. She should have first come to see him so that he could talk to Stephen if needed.

The next day Stephen is playing video games with three friends in his room and gets a hang-up call from a girl, saying "You're stupid." Surrounded by his friends, he calls Samantha, thinking it's her, and gets instead the mom's answering machine and leaves a threatening message. He hangs up and the boys start laughing. The molehill has now become a mountain.

The next day Samantha's mom calls us and tells us everything that's happened. We are horrified by Stephen's prank call and frightened by Mrs. Osman's "pure rage" on the playground — she tells us she'd imagined Stephen lying dying at the side of the road and honestly wondered if she'd even stop to help. We are further horrified when she tells us that somehow Marsha Dimone heard about the prank call, told the O'Neils about it, and both families came over to encourage her to call the police and report it. She wishes she had called us first, before the police, and apologizes.

We agree to get together to meet as two families at our house that afternoon. It's a surprisingly wonderful meeting. Stephen apologizes and hands Samantha's mom his letter of apology for the prank call; and apologizes to Samantha for eating her lunch. Samantha's older brother apologizes for teasing Stephen about having two moms (which Stephen has never told us – like so much else we learn only through others). Samantha's dad looks at us and says, "It's so unfair. He's become the lightning rod for everything that anyone doesn't like at that school." (We agree with him but are very surprised that a white man "gets it.") We ask him how he knows about this phenomenon of lightning rods. He tells us he's Turkish and the son of a migrant worker. He attended school in Germany and was often the target of kids' rage about other things. Once he was almost drowned.

The meeting ends with the feeling that we have each found new friends. Mrs. Osman says she's going to try to cancel the complaint to the police. She calls two days later to say it's too late — the complaint has already been written up and Stephen will be investigated. The police are coming over the next day.

The next day we have a good two-hour conversation with the policeman. Stephen shows him a copy of the letter of apology he gave Mrs. Osman. The policeman says the incident should go no further, since we are very clear about the danger of such calls, Stephen has apologized and the family wants in any case to withdraw the complaint. He's just got to write up the incident and that will be the end of it.

As the policeman is leaving, we ask him to please mention the fact of the earlier prank call to Stephen and that the mom had yelled at Stephen on the playground, so it won't seem that Stephen's call was entirely random or unprovoked. The policeman heaves a sigh, sits down again, and complains he doesn't have time to write a book. We say we don't want a book, just a few lines of background, not to excuse in any way what Stephen did, but just to note that it wasn't entirely out of the blue — we don't want to play into stereotypes of "Black Boys Are Inherently Violent." The policeman reluctantly agrees to add some context to the report on Stephen's behavior and leaves.

A few days later I call Samantha's mom as we'd agreed, to let her know how the meeting with the policeman went. She answers the phone and upon hearing my voice starts screaming, "I never want to talk with you again ... and I've told my husband and kids never to speak to you again ... no reconciliation is possible!" I ask her what on earth this is about. She screams, "You know good and well what this is about." I say, "If it's about adding some context to the report on Stephen's behavior, you can understand why." She continues to scream that she won't talk to me and I finally say, "Okay, then, good-bye."

I am completely shaken. How did we get from being new friends to becoming eternal enemies?

I call the policeman. He says he never spoke to Mrs. Osman and that what he writes is none of her business, but that "no reconciliation is possible" (the exact phrase used by Mrs. Osman). I ask for a copy of his report. He says he'll send it. We wait two weeks and call again. No response. Instead, three weeks later, we get a document in the mail headed "Official Notice to Appear/Juvenile Probation Department." I call the policeman and he says, "It will put some fear in Stephen and that's a good thing." We ask, "What about your saying it would go no further?" He repeats that putting some fear into Stephen is a good thing. I tell him Stephen is already so fearful he isn't sleeping at night (a problem that had gone away years ago and is now back). He needs no more fear! What on earth did he put in the police report that has led to probation, and why haven't we gotten the report?

He says he can't give us the report. We have to go ask Maria in the city police department. I call and Maria says to come down to the office. I explain that I work more than full-time, but Maria is adamant. I go down the next day, but now Maria is off for three weeks and will return after Stephen's probation meeting has already occurred. The main desk tells me to fill out a "Request for Juvenile Probation Report" and take it four towns away to the judge in the county seat, see if he's in, and ask him to sign a release. I ask them to at least fax me the "Request for Juvenile Probation Report" form, but they insist I come into the office to get it. I take the next day off work to run around for all this, beginning with the city office where I am to pick up the form they refuse to fax me.

The main desk there says, "Oh you don't need that form from us. Your son is the perpetrator not the victim. You have to get a special form from the judge and you have to go down to the county seat for that." I say, "Well, since you're the ones who told me to come here instead of there, can you at least call there and find out if the person you are telling me to talk to is actually there and will give me the form?" They say they cannot do this. I ask if they will give me the phone number so I can do it. They have no phone number for the right office in the county seat. I can't imagine that this is possible. Surely they have more of a clue than I do?

At this point, I start crying. My life seems completely hopeless. A molehill has become a mountain range and I just can't climb it. Another woman in the city office who's overheard this whole exchange takes pity on me. She asks to borrow my cell phone — for some reason she can't make this call on a city line — and calls the courthouse and learns the judge is off for the day.

I can't stop crying. I tell her I've taken the whole day off work today, must I take tomorrow off too? She tells me the only thing to do is to get a lawyer to go to court for me. I finally stop crying, thank her profusely and spend the rest of the day getting a lawyer.

Two days and $500 later, we have the report and it's a shock. Mrs. Osman's behavior is reported as simply *our feeling* that she behaved that way, not as the fact that the principal reported this exact behavior of hers to the police. In addition, our "feelings" about her are written up to prove that we aren't taking this matter seriously. Claims that Stephen is a bully (words straight from the mouths of Marsha Dimone and Joann O'Neil, which Mrs. Osman had said she was sorry she'd bought into) are written up as fact. The final shock of this report comes with the last line. Despite the policeman's reassurance that in his experience a case like this will go no further, he concludes with the words "RECOMMENDATION: Juvenile Review." Hence Stephen's probation hearing.

At this point, Stacy and I are looking at the mountain range that has grown out of a molehill and wonder if we are going to be dead before we can get our children raised or if they will be dead no matter what we can manage to do. We have spent many hours talking to friends, including lawyers and people in our two churches, and have heard everything from "Every big African-American boy in this town has got a police report" to "It's impossible to raise anybody, white or Black, to be healthy here," "You won't win a pissing contest with the police," "The cops have the power and you don't. They can lie and they do lie. Even in this town ..." and "The best hope for African-American kids is good schools and you won't find them better than here!"

Stephen's teacher, who is a lawyer and an incredibly sympathetic ally, tells us to read *Kill Them*

Before They Grow[8], which echoes our own experiences with chilling accuracy. The teacher is thrilled we've discovered *Yo, Little Brother...*[9] and we feel it's wonderful he already knows about it.

I call the community liaison in the police department. We would like some help with Stephen's imminent probation hearing and the context that created it: our interactions with the O'Neils, Marsha Dimone and now the Osman family. We need to sit down together somehow with these families that have problems with Stephen and with us, problems that they take into their own hands. Our next-door neighbor has called the phenomenon "vigilantism," and that word does capture the terrifying aspect it has for us. Any decision by a teacher, principal, superintendent or police officer that these families don't agree with, they retry, convicting us without a hearing, and carrying out appalling gossip-mongering sentences that have cost us many weeks of heartache and, most of all, threaten our son. They project "bully" on him unremittingly, yet they are the ones bullying him and us. It's been going on for years, and the only miracle we pray for now is that the accusation "Stephen is a bully" won't become a self-fulfilling prophecy.

---

[8] *Kill Them Before They Grow: Misdiagnosis of African-American Boys in American Classrooms* by Michael Porter, African-American Images, 1998.

[9] *Yo, Little Brother...: Basic Rules of Survival for Young African-American Males* by Anthony Davis and Jeffrey Jackson, African-American Images, 1998. (In 2007, Volume II of this book was published.)

We call the community liaison again, as he hasn't called back. Again, he doesn't call back. I write him. He doesn't reply. Time marches on and we find ourselves marching into the probation department. Stephen is sentenced to two weeks of anti-violence classes. I rage inwardly, *What about making the adults in this violent community take these classes?*

We take Stephen out of school for two weeks while we sort out how to keep him safe from these families and their hatred. It's incredibly hard because of our demanding jobs, but friends, family and neighbors watch out for him and us during this bad time.

Interestingly enough, with Stephen out of the picture, the mixed-race boy in the classroom is now the target of suspicion and stories. We learn this from a friend of the Osmans who calls us to tell us, very disturbed at what's happened with our family.

For years I will wonder what happened in this situation that Stacy and I call "the molehill that adults turned into a mountain range." The simple explanation, which my white privilege has blinded me to, is that the policeman, upset that we'd asked him to add context to his report, discussed our request with Mrs. Osman before writing it, enraged her, and then lied to us about the whole thing. A second possibility is that someone in the police force — maybe another member of the homophobic church — is tipping off Marsha Dimone about anything that happens with our family, and she keeps everyone else informed. A third possibility and a fourth ... I'm driving myself crazy trying to figure this out. With no help or even response from those empowered to help us, I feel like I am in a Kafkaesque world, where bizarre things happen to us for no reason that we can ever discover.

Whatever happened, it takes years more effort trying to work with the police before I will admit the obvious: The police have not only failed to protect my family, but they have further enflamed all parties and endangered us all. This is in addition to wearing Stacy and me down with endless run-arounds. Is this deliberate or do they just need better training? Or have they been trained to act like this when there are African-Americans involved? (We know that in the neighboring town officers are instructed to stop, question and if possible search all Black people. Years later, we will learn that this has also been a policy in our own police department — in fact, the police chief will have to leave when it's discovered.)

Oh, That's So Gay

STACY

I'm in a sports store shopping for soccer shoes for Stephen. Two young middle-school boys, 10 or 11, come up behind me to look at the shoes. One sees a pair he likes, but the other says to him, "No way, those shoes are *so* gay." The other kid is startled and quickly loses interest in those shoes, focusing on another pair.

I stand there and wonder if I'm going to say anything. Since I am a diversity consultant, this is the work I do all the time. The work is rewarding ... and also tiring at times. I think I deserve a break when I'm just in a store shopping.

Still .... I turn to the boy who made the comment and say, "You know, when you say something like 'Oh, that's so gay,' do you understand what you are saying and the impact it might have on others?"

His buddy says, "I didn't say it, I didn't say it."

The boy who made the remark just looks at me with a mixture of shock and anger.

I say, "That is a derogatory comment aimed at lesbians and gay men, and it hurts."

The boy replies, "I didn't really mean it."

"If that's true, why did you say it?"

"All the kids say it ... we're just joking."

I explain about the difference between what he intends and what the impact might be, and point out that joking about this kind of thing really isn't funny.

He shrugs, and they both walk off.

I think, *What's up with this? We are in the year 2001 and kids still are saying "You're so gay" as a way of embarrassing and controlling each other through peer pressure?*

As I walk up to the cash register, the two boys are heading toward the door. The one who had made the comment says very loudly, "Oh, that is so *homosexual*."

The Towers Fall, Hatred Rises

STACY

We are awakened at 6:30 a.m. by our daughter, who tells us to turn on CNN, a plane has just flown into a building. As we watch the screen, we see the second plane crash into the second tower of the World Trade Center. We are shocked, numbed, terrified. I feel like I'm watching scenes from the movie *Independence Day*.

We stay glued to the TV for hours. Not long after the twin towers and the Pentagon are hit, President Bush and others come on screen and talk about "evil people" and "cowards." I'm very suspicious of words that demonize, that steer people's hearts and minds away from inquiring into what has really occurred. Cowards? Somehow, flying into a building and losing your life for something you passionately believe in doesn't strike me as cowardice. It's many other things, certainly, but not cowardice. (Bill Maher will say as much on his show *Politically Incorrect* and lose many of his sponsors ... and finally, his job.)

Within a matter of hours, Arabs and Muslims become targets of harassment and violence across the U.S. If you look like the evil enemy — dark, foreign, mysterious, unknown — you become suspect. Your life has just become full of danger and fear. The nurse in our doctor's office is Iranian. She tells me several patients stopped coming to our doctor because of her. The young Arab man at our local Blockbuster is shot. Lots of people are comparing these kinds of events to the interning of the Japanese in the 1940s.

Arab-Americans, Muslim-Americans, and any visitors who could be mistaken for Arabs and/or Muslims, have suddenly become "the enemy." Hundreds of them are detained. I think, *Timothy McVeigh did not inspire this kind of response when he blew up the Federal Building in Oklahoma City. Why not?*

McVeigh was seen as an individual having committed a solo act with a little help. No one saw him as representative of all white people. No one assumed that all other white people thought like him and could do what he did. We didn't round up white people by the hundreds on the chance that they might be material witnesses. We didn't stop frequenting restaurants and other businesses owned or run by white people. We didn't attack white people or make them afraid to leave their homes. We didn't indiscriminately tell white people that we were uncomfortable having them as passengers on our planes and ask them to get off.

Why the difference? Is it because the bombing in Oklahoma City resulted in less loss of life? Is it because we saw McVeigh as an aberration, an anomaly, with no far-reaching implications of his behavior? Is it because McVeigh was a homegrown white boy that we somehow couldn't quite believe he did it, even though we did execute him? Is it because we think it's preposterous to consider willy-nilly arresting or persecuting white people because there are so many of them and how could you possibly know who was who?

Or is it simply that we find it easier to demonize, dehumanize, and kill those who are darker, stranger, non-Christian, more the "other" than the white, mostly Christian people in charge of the police, the government, the banks and the schools? And easier still to label those of us who ask these questions as "unpatriotic" because we do ask, because we aren't waving flags but are inquiring into the possible seeds of terrorism, because we are grief-stricken at all the horror and devastation of war and want

Funny How We're All Americans Now
STACY

Our friend Yolanda, who's African-American, sends out an email after 9/11. She includes an article about the need for the U.S. to unite in the war against terrorism and the "destruction of evil." It calls on every American's sense of patriotism and pride to join the war and fight the enemy.

The article makes no distinction when it refers to "Americans." All are included. Yolanda's sole comment/question about the article is, "Isn't it funny that when we are being called to risk our lives, we're no longer "African-American" but just "American"?

This calls to mind a scene from the movie *A Time to Kill* when the defendant, played by Black actor Samuel L. Jackson, says to his white lawyer, "This country is in a war, and you and I are on different sides."

I wonder what it would feel like if your experience in this country was that you already had metaphorical bombs landing on aspects of your life most of the time — the bombs of racist, sexist, homophobic, xenophobic thoughts and behavior that did incredible damage, including killing — and now you were being asked to step up to defend the very country whose climate gives rise to bombs like those falling on your own head?

Beautiful Baez
STACY

It's a Sunday afternoon and there's a gathering of people in the downtown area of our city. People of various faiths, nationalities, races, ages, all there to express solidarity, to rekindle a sense of hope in the weeks after 9/11. Prayers, songs, poems are offered up. A young man steps to the microphone and begins intoning a beautiful, haunting Islamic chant. The echoes waft across the entire quad. A powerful statement about how the religion of Islam is not the problem.

Joan Baez comes to the mike and her crystal clear, wondrous voice fills the air. I don't even remember what she sang. "Amazing Grace," I think. Suddenly, I am thrown back in time, remembering when I'd heard first that voice, a voice that sang protest songs but promised a future, a new day.

This afternoon we all experience that the human spirit in its purest form will not capitulate to rage and violence because it is the nature of this spirit to love and be loved. We are reminded by all who speak and sing that we need to make every effort to keep this reality at the forefront of all we do to bring about peace.

Celebration: Our 25th
STACY

We invite friends and family to attend our 25th anniversary of being a couple. My two cousins come up from Southern California to help prepare for the event. I grew up with these two women and we were very close until I came out as a lesbian. After a long period of estrangement, we were able to find common ground and rekindle our relationship. They do a wonderful job; they're both gifted in the art of celebration and presentation.

To say this event brought together different worlds would be an understatement. People from our work, friends from 12-step programs, my parents, aunts, and cousins, Barb's sister …. The smiling faces are white, Black, Asian, and Latino. There are little people — one who at 4-foot, 2-inches will soon become a national name — gay, bisexual, transgender, straight, upper class, middle class, lower class, young and old, all gathered under one roof at the Unitarian church down the street from our house. Allies and advocates everywhere.

The Greeks fill one huge table, which I think is miraculous. If someone had told me 10 years ago that this would happen, no way would I have believed it. I miss one immediate and dear family member who later tells me that coming to our celebration would have violated her Christian values. (It will be a few more years before we work on our relationship and can discuss this experience.)

People have often asked me how I can be around my Greek family of origin, given their homophobia and racism. It's true that they have struggled with Barb and me as a couple, and with our having Black children. There have been excruciating times throughout the years, but the reason I hang in with them is that they hang in with me, and theirs is the harder job, I believe. Look at them all here today! I am so happy and grateful.

The food is wonderful. We've laid out quite a spread, and people have brought favorite dishes to share, awesome food from different cultures. After the meal, certain people we've asked to say something get up and speak, read poems, and sing. Barb and I are very moved and humbled by what we hear. Barb's sister speaks, representing Barb's entire family back East. Barb and I speak, too, and then I sing a song I wrote for her on our 10th anniversary.

We do "open mike" now and invite anyone to come up and share whatever they'd like. One person talks about how her experiences of loving and being loved have impacted her life. Others follow, with love being the central theme. There are some incredible stories.

Suddenly, my dad stands up at his table in the back of the room. He starts walking to the microphone. I'm stunned. And very nervous. Up until the last minute he said he wasn't coming, that Barb's and my relationship "just isn't right." The room turns quiet. He looks at me, smiles, takes the microphone, and starts to speak. "I can't believe what a wonderful group of people this is." His voice cracks, he begins crying, and through his tears says, "I'm so proud. I'm very, very proud of my daughter. I wish I had friends like this." I start to cry. I hug my father and whisper "Thank you" in his ear. Through the years, he and I have had a very tumultuous relationship. But in this moment, I feel something shift.

When I look up again, I see that others are crying, too. There is something about a parent reaching beyond himself to support a child that touches people deeply, especially after a long period of struggle, especially when there are so many lesbian, gay, bisexual, and transgendered people who haven't had that acknowledgment and support. To those people we say, you never know — even when you think you do. People are never too old to change, and you can't predict what it will be that can turn that river around.

Afterwards, we move the tables and the dancing begins. We have an amazing disc jockey who plays everything from Greek to R&B. At one point, Barb and I look around at everyone dancing and say to each other, "This is a miracle!" It feels a little surreal: doing a Greek line dance and then segueing into Aretha Franklin's "Respect"!

Talk About Being a Family

STACY

Barb and I are asked to talk about being a family during a service at our Unitarian church. This is after 9/11, and it strikes us that now people may want to break down old barriers and listen more carefully to those among us who may not fit the usual church attendee profile.

It is a lovely experience. It feels like people listen to and appreciate what we have to say. After we speak, other families with non-traditional configurations — mixed, blended, adopted — share their experiences. One Iranian man tells how he and his family are now being targeted in the larger community and how he fears leaving their house. Out of that sharing, a resolution is endorsed to be on call for this family or any other that needs support to go out. If you call anyone on the list, someone will show up at your house to accompany the whole family or any member of it anywhere they need to go.

Dance, Dance, Dance

STACY

Since the time she could walk, Shawna's gift for dancing has been evident. The girl has an ability to move, and when a good piece of dance music comes on, she rocks out. Whenever she takes the dance floor, all eyes are on her. She does okay with formal dance (tap, ballet), but the scripted-ahead-of-time aspect of it doesn't really interest her. Turn on her favorite radio station and it's another story entirely.

When Shawna is 14, we go to my nephew's wedding in Colorado. My nephew is marrying a non-Greek, so the music played at the wedding reception is quite eclectic — it ranges from Greek dancing to Western line dancing. Shawna is hanging out with her cousin (my niece) and a young Black woman who is the cousin's best friend. The girls look bored until the DJ puts on a great hip-hop tune. Shawna immediately jumps up, flings off her shoes, and hits the dance floor. The other two girls join her and they dance, overjoyed that finally "their" music is being played.

Later, one of the men watching the dancers points at Shawna and says to me, "That's the most beautiful woman I've ever seen. I can't stop looking at her dancing. She's absolutely mesmerizing!"

"Yes," I say, "and she's my daughter, and she's 14."

He sputters in his beer and says, "Oh ... well, she sure is a good dancer," and moves away.

She sure is.

George's 'Your Job Is ... '

BARB

George is one of the most brilliant people in my company. He sparkles when he talks, and he listens so deeply I soon hear myself say interesting things. One night on a bus coming home from an offsite meeting, he tells me his people were known as the Jews of India — always being expelled, moved out, moved on.

Several weeks later I walk downstairs to George's cubicle to bring him a book I've ordered for him: Amartya Sen's *Development as Freedom*.[10] This Nobel-prize winning economist from Bangladesh argues that the way the West measures development — our own and that of other countries — ensures we will never fully develop. Tracking back to the classical economists, he picks up threads that were dropped along the way and argues that true development is not measured by gross national product but by the extent to which the country's people enjoy different kinds of freedom.

One of the kinds of freedom is the freedom to live out the 70 years of an allotted life uninterrupted by death through preventable disease or violence. In one chart that I am showing George, you can see that among males, white infants born in the U.S. have the highest life expectancy. The next highest group is infant males born in China, followed by infant males born in Kerala, India. The final group

---

[10] Knopf, 2001

compared on this chart has the lowest life
expectancy. This group is African-American males
born in the U.S.

With surprising anguish and even more
surprising tears — we're now standing in the hall by
the water cooler — I say to George, "My son and I
live in different countries. I live in a highly developed
one. He lives in a very undeveloped one, one that is
dangerous for him, one in which he is not expected
to reach age 70."

George does not flinch, or pull back, or look
around to see who's witnessing this scene. With
gentle compassion, he says, without missing a beat,
"Barb, have you ever considered that your job may
be to help your son emigrate from the undeveloped
country to the developed country? I speak as an
immigrant. Having come from India, I know that this
is a job. Do you think with your help he might be
able to 'emigrate'?"

Suddenly I feel washed with hope. I am not alone;
I am understood; and here is a new way of looking at
something terrible so it's not so impossible. Of
course, the point isn't that Stephen becomes white.
The point is to teach him how to behave in a way
that white people won't be afraid of him. (I recall our
Jewish neighbors advising us to get Stephen glasses,
even though he doesn't need them, so that he'll look
bookish, a scholar, and less like whatever else his
tormenters think he is.)

This is a fine line, a difficult balancing act.
Without giving up and totally assimilating, he needs
to know how to keep the spotlight off himself, how to

keep from being targeted. He needs to know the "rules" intimately so he can follow them, particularly when his life depends on it. When he completely knows the rules, and when and how to follow them to protect himself, then he will learn how and when to appropriately break the rules in order to be authentic, to be fully himself, without incurring punishment. I have great faith that my son has the capacity to learn and apply these distinctions. I just want there to be enough time to teach him before I die, or before he does.

Four years after our conversation about immigration and my son, George dies, tragically, of brain cancer. I meet his son at the funeral. His son is 16 and profoundly autistic. He is excited about the party, wondering when his father is going to be here. I am struck anew by how much George knew about living in different countries under the same roof, about the uphill climb of helping a child emigrate from a place of danger to one of relative safety. I am struck anew by how much we all have in common, how much we have to teach each other, and how hard life can be.

PART III:
THE TEEN YEARS

Nightmare Times

BARB

High school has begun and our daughter is in the ninth grade. This is considered to be one of the top high schools in the area and within the country.

The first big challenge for Shawna is that school is not fun. Highly academic, it focuses on kids aiming for a prestigious four-year college. This leaves all but the brightest of the conventionally bright kids falling through the cracks.

Shawna is hanging with a dozen girls. About half are African-American, and half are white. Within one year, one girl runs away, another tries to kill herself, another gets involved in a prostitution ring and gets pregnant, two are raped, another brings a BB gun to school and shoots at two girls she doesn't like, and all of them are sneaking out in the middle of the night to meet boys or men — some of whom they've met on the Internet.

What is going on? It seems as if these kids are trying to do themselves in, one way or another. The most frightening thing? They seem unaffected by it all. It's as if this is merely an extension of the violence they see in the media, hear in music, and witness in the world.

We're terrified that our daughter could be killed by what she's doing.

Three Choices

STACY

I'm talking with my friend, Marsha, whom I've worked with and known for a long time. We're talking about the kids and I'm filling her in on the latest. I tell her that no matter what we do, it doesn't seem to really make a difference.

I ask Marsha (who's Black) what options she thinks we have in terms of raising these kids.

She says, "You can raise Black kids to lie low and not encourage them too much so as to avoid getting crushed. Or you can raise them with self-confidence, self-esteem, pride, and high expectations — and let the culture crush them. Or you can await a period of awakening, like the Harlem Renaissance, or Civil Rights, where Black dignity and pride arise for a moment in time before things revert to where they were."

I'm not sure what to do with this input ... but it sounds exactly right. And very disturbing.

Raising Girls, Raising Boys: Lots of Lies, Lots of Noise

BARB

Here we are, two lesbian feminists, having to admit that our experience of raising our teenage daughter is profoundly different — and in ways much more difficult — than raising our teen-age son (so far).

Testosterone has a way of putting things out there, so to speak. With boys, it seems like what you see is what you get. If they're angry and act it out, there it is. If they go speeding around town on their bicycles with no helmets, you hear about it. When they get their licenses and go dragging down streets, the parents know who they are and call the police.

Teenage girls can certainly do all those things, too. But there is something else operating that is very different. There's a constant sneaking around and lying, masked by smiley faces and cooperation. Much more than the boys, the girls seem to go "underground," living two parallel lives. It's the sweet smile that hides the night-before activity of being on the Internet, setting up meeting times with grown men, sneaking out at night to hook up with friends and the men they are meeting.

The sun may be shining, but you can feel the premonitions, the intuitions, the deep knowing that something is going on that is definitely not good, that is terribly dangerous.

Sexual Battery?

BARB

It's 6 p.m. and I've just come home from a 12-hour day at work. I'm beat and ready to be done! Wrong. The phone rings.

It's Stephen's principal. He sounds excited when he asks, "Have the police come there yet?"

I say, "No, what is this about?"

"Oh, you don't know? Well, you're going to find out soon. I think I've got him! This time I think I've got him!"

Feeling my stomach lurch, I say, "Phil, what are you talking about?"

It seems that Stephen was waiting in a long line at the office to use the phone, in his case to call home so we'd pick him up. He doesn't want to walk home today. Waiting in line, he bumps the butt of the girl in front of him. When she gets home she tells her mother that a Black boy touched her butt. The mother calls the principal to complain. The principal believes this to be a case of sexual battery and has called the police to investigate and they will be at our home shortly.

Three officers soon knock on the door and we invite them in. They speak to Stephen and ask him what happened? He tells them he accidentally bumped this girl while they were waiting in a line too long for the office, all squashed together. They explain to us that there is an allegation of sexual battery and they will have to investigate.

The questioning of 11 witnesses fails to corroborate the accusation of sexual battery. Sexual battery requires premeditation, sexual thrill as a motive, and explicit touching of the genitals. As one officer tells us, "If we had to investigate sexual battery every time a 12-year-old boy bumps into a girl, we'd have to shut down the department. Let me guess. He's the kind of kid that would rather be playing video games." We laugh and confirm that fact.

This same officer stays awhile and we talk. He tells us, "I'll be honest. I'm getting pressure from the department to write this up to support the principal. I'm staying out of the office till I submit the report of the investigation ... You should get him out of that school. He's being targeted ... You should move out of this town, you will never make it here."

We ask him where we could move or what there is about this town that is so much worse than where he lives, for example. He shares with us a comparison: In the recent floods, he was assigned duty by the sandbag pit, where we all went to bag sand in case our homes flooded. His job was to make sure residents of our town didn't hit each other as they scrambled to fill the most bags before the sand ran out. I recall having been shoved out of the way by a guy with a bigger shovel, and I thank this fine officer for having doing this duty. He continues. In his town, up in the mountains, all the townspeople bag the sand, people take what they need, and bags are delivered to those unable to get out to pick them up or to fill them at all. The main restaurant stays open 24/7 for free coffee to all the folks bagging sand. "That's the difference," he says, and invites us to move to his town.

We ask him if there are any Blacks in his town. He smiles ruefully and concedes there are not.

After the officer's report finding "no cause" is submitted, the principal calls us to say that the report notwithstanding, he wants to proceed with a hearing to suspend or expel our son, and he has the full support of the assistant superintendent of schools.

I call the assistant superintendent and ask him if in fact he supports this hearing. He gets quite upset and says, "I told him no way, if the police report doesn't support the allegation." He continues, "It's his right as a principal to hold the hearing anyway, but it's against my advice."

The day of the hearing arrives. Stephen is supposed to attend. The three of us walk in and around the table are the principal, the assistant principal, the school counselor, the dean, the African-American assistant and Stephen's teacher. It is daunting.

The principal opens the meeting by saying, "I understand from the assistant superintendent that you've agreed to this meeting only if I am not present. Therefore I will remove myself after Stephen talks about what he's done and leave you with my staff" (all of whom report to him).

The hearing commences with Stephen confessing the crime of bumping into a girl waiting in line. I then stand to leave the room with him. The principal becomes agitated and says, "No, he is supposed to be here for this meeting." Well," I say, "his uncle, who is African-American and a state-award winning body builder and former probation officer, and who lettered in all five sports at this very high school, is in the front office to take him home, and that is what he's going to do. I do not want Stephen present for any more of this shameful meeting."

When I return, the principal has left. And Stacy and I talk about how horrifying it is that the people there to protect and model responsible behavior for our son have brought us to this meeting. We believe any of them that have had a role in this trumped-up charge should be ashamed of themselves.

We leave the room and the staff votes unanimously not to support their boss in suspending or expelling our son. This is incredibly heroic of them.

The principal returns and says, "I understand my staff has voted to allow Stephen to remain in school. I will do so on two conditions: one, that Stephen not be seen on campus by this girl ever again; and two, that you parents show me more trust and respect with regard to how I deal with your son."

We reply that since Stephen is the largest kid on campus and one of the few African-Americans, it is a set-up to make it a condition for his attending school that he not be seen by this girl. (Especially because, as we've learned from two of Stephen's friends and had validated by one of the investigating officers, she is trying to connect with him, in that fumbling way of budding pre-pubescent attraction.) On the second point, we state flatly that we have no trust or respect at all for this principal. And in fact, we do not believe Stephen is safe at this school with a principal so obviously out to get him. Since the law guarantees an education that is harassment-free and appropriate to the child's abilities, we would like to know what alternative school they would suggest.

We get a call within two hours from one of the staff telling us to pick our choice: The district will transfer him anywhere we want, including a private school. We have made noises about a lawsuit and wonder if this is what's driving this offer.

We choose a private school, as expensive as the nearby private university, which specializes in impulse control and includes very bright kids.

Stephen is very upset. "I didn't do anything!" We say, "Yes, you did. You accidentally touched the rear end of a girl. As a big Black boy and soon to be big Black man, you can be killed for that. We are sending you where you will learn one hundred percent impulse control so that you never again accidentally touch anyone."

What? Our Son Good at Math?

BARB

Stephen starts seventh grade at the private school. He hates the school from the first, as most kids would if they were yanked out of their old school and away from their friends. However, in the first year, he jumps four grade levels, from fourth to eighth grade math. For the first time, his forte is math. Who knew? He also has a wonderful Black male therapist who helps him to understand the power of choice: choosing to fulfill others' expectations of him as a criminal, or wow them that he's not. That's the upside. The downside is that Stephen hates his seventh- and eighth-grade years, doesn't see the point, doesn't participate in a single after-school activity, doesn't bring home one friend nor respond to one invitation to go home to someone's house.

The Wonder of Wilderness

STACY

Fifteen-year-old Shawna defies the curfews and breaks the rules we've set to afford her some measure of safety. She and her friends have no idea how much danger they are in sneaking out after curfew — or not coming in at all. We know Shawna is walking a thin line between safety and danger and that any small thing can push her over the edge into terrifying territory. We try talking to her. It doesn't work. We ask other adults she likes to talk to her. Doesn't work. We ask some of her more mature friends to talk to her. That doesn't work either. She is in the *grippa*, as we Greeks say, and we can't loosen the rope around her neck.

We consult with all kinds of people. Other parents, our close friends, certain family members, a therapist. Nothing seems to help us — or her — in terms of loosening the grip of her peer group and their collective and dangerous decisions.

Then we start talking with educational professionals who deal with teens and come up with options for dealing with serious situations. We finally find two educational consultants, wonderful women in Oregon, and after hours and hours of conversation and research, they come up with a wilderness camp in Utah they feel will work for our daughter. We rush through a second mortgage on our house so we can afford the camp.

But still ...Utah? Mormon country?

The women point out that Mormons have the troubled-teen industry sewn up. "Yes, there will be Mormons at the wilderness camp," they admit. "They own this one and all the other good ones, but not all Mormons are out to convert you or have lived completely sheltered lives. "

In fact, the Mormon counselor they recommend is a lesbian who's been excommunicated from the Mormon church. The Mormon social worker turns out to be a recent convert who confides to us that she married her handsome husband for himself, but she also wanted to marry into the faith for the extended family and church structure to help her with her teenage kids from a previous marriage. We are chastened by having to look at our own unthinking prejudice — yet *again!*

A dear friend, a brother to us, Gerald, is in the business of transporting people who have to be taken from one place to another, even when they don't want to be. Like our daughter.

Gerald gives us the game plan for the nerve-wracking event that's about to take place. First, he and his female business partner will come to our home at 5 a.m. They want us and our son out of the house. They say this will greatly reduce the drama. So we have Stephen stay overnight at a friend's, give Gerald a key, and plan to get in the car and park around the corner just before the arranged time. Gerald explains that he and his partner, Lucia, will wake Shawna up, have her dress quickly, and take her to the airport where they will fly out to Salt Lake City. People from the wilderness camp will meet them and take Shawna to base headquarters where she will be admitted.

We follow Gerald's instructions, and the thing I remember most is sitting in our car sobbing our eyes out. The pain of this is indescribable. Gerald calls us when they are out of the house, and we go home to collapse. After crying more, smoking more cigarettes, and trying to tell ourselves we had to do this, that there was no choice, we try to get some sleep, totally exhausted.

Living Past 30

BARB

We're in Puerto Vallarta, Mexico, on vacation with Granny and her grandsons. Shawna is still in wilderness camp and we miss her so much, especially when we go to her favorite places. We meet an African-American couple from Las Vegas at some hotel event and continue to see them on and off during the week.

At checkout time, we're chatting with the woman as her husband checks out. We start talking about kids and mention that part of our extended African-American family is with us. Quickly, as the checkout moves forward, we go deep. We share with her our experiences being the kind of family we are. We talk about the particular challenge of raising Black boys, particularly getting them to adulthood before they are imprisoned or killed. We talk about Mary's son who was murdered at 26 in a drive-by shooting less than 10 minutes from where we live, across the freeway. So close, yet a world apart from the affluent town we live in. We say we've known Mary for six years and this was the first time, on this trip, that she ever spoke about what happened to her son, Frank.

This woman, who's a bit younger than we are, looks at us with no surprise. With sadness in her eyes, she tells us that her husband's 17-year-old son was murdered a year ago in Las Vegas. The police called it a suicide so they wouldn't have to investigate. Her husband carries his grief and rage with him all the time, and the Mexican sun and margaritas have done nothing to lighten his burden.

She now moves to the front desk to sign something, and we begin talking with the guy behind us, a handsome young Black man born in Panama. He and his wife have been living in Austin, Texas, for a while because of his work. They plan on starting a family, and he says they will either move back to Panama or else come to Puerto Vallarta. He doesn't want his children brought up in the U.S.

"It's no place to raise kids," he tells us.

Seeing the Light

STACY

As the days and weeks of wilderness camp go by, Shawna, now 16 (having had her birthday at camp), emerges as an "emotional leader" in her group. The counselors tell us she is doing very well. They don't tell her, or us, when she will be able to come home. They say they'll call us a couple of days before, and our daughter won't know until we pick her up. They explain that this ensures the kids stay in the present and don't get too preoccupied about when they will leave.

The phone call comes six weeks later. We fly in and stay at a motel overnight before we'll pick her up the next day. The motel we stay at is run by Mormons. In fact, this whole little town is Mormon except for the owners of the motel, who are Catholic. Our prejudices humming along, we are nervous about our stay. Then, the woman who owns the motel with her husband tells us her own story about a troubled daughter. She gives Barb a pendant of the Virgin Mary and a prayer card, tearfully explaining that she prayed the prayer on the card and wore the necklace every day, and it helped her, and it will help Barb.

Barb brings the necklace with the Virgin Mary back to the room to show me, but suddenly her face changes and she runs out of the room. She goes back to the motel owner to point out to this kind woman that she's somehow gotten the wrong necklace. This isn't the Virgin Mary; it's the Virgin of Guadalupe, the Black Madonna. Did she know our daughter was Black? The woman smiles sweetly and says she didn't know our daughter was Black or even that she owned such a medal, but clearly it is the one Barb is meant to have. This necklace remains among

Barb's cherished possessions. Prayer and wearing it does give comfort and help.

The owner of a restaurant across the street from the motel brings a wonderful meal to our room. We talk to other people who speak of how they converted to Mormonism because of the focus on family and community.

We are finding that our lives, and that of our child, depend on Mormons. And they are caring and loving with us. There is definitely a feeling of being connected and a sense of family being the priority. One man shares that he converted to Mormonism after he came to this small town. Four years ago, his wife died after a protracted bout with terminal cancer. Three years ago, his two kids, ages 20 and 19, were killed in a head-on collision with a drunk driver. The man had nothing left and was very despondent. The Mormons in the town gave him money to start a business, and he met a Mormon woman he cared for. He converted and ended up marrying her in the Mormon Church. This man talked about his skepticism about the Mormon faith and said there were some things he still had difficulty with. But he also said that he'd never been treated so wonderfully and compassionately, and he is finally healing from his own tragedies. He and his wife may adopt — and the Mormon Church will pay the adoption expenses if they need that help.

We get it. How wonderful it would be to have this kind of support system in this life.

Shawna is beyond thrilled to see us, and we her. We can't stop crying, any of us. She has changed dramatically. Six weeks without a cell phone or any of her peer group, six weeks under the stars, in clear air, walking, camping, thinking, reflecting. She will tell us in later years she hated it — and it saved her life. After we get home, we notice the wild sneaking out is over, and we are now having discussions about her plans, whether for an evening or a year. She certainly knows how to make a fire using two sticks and demonstrates this new skill to anyone who doubts it!

Special Ed Night

BARB

Back-to-School night at Shawna's high school. I sit through the eager teachers explaining to the note-taking parents of the Ivy-League-bound how to ensure their kids get into the gifted and advanced classes. I wonder if there are others in the room who wish we could talk about how to help kids with learning disabilities master basic academic skills. The No Child Left Behind program was allocated no money by the Bush government (which mandated it), so Vocational Education has been gutted and the money redirected to getting everybody to college. I wonder if anyone else wonders what kind of work their child should be training for and where they will get the training or the motivation to pursue it.

I can't wait to get to the classroom where I'll be with the other parents whose kids are in Special Ed. This is Shawna's first year in such a program and so far it's been a disaster. Most of the kids feel — and are perceived by many students and some staff —

like rejects and are acting out, at best, by smoking dope and skipping school.

Now I'm here. I look around the room and I'm so proud of us. As we all gather in, and before things start officially, I say, "Well, here we are. The special parents ... the true heroes ...." The teacher nods. A few other parents look down at their notebooks. Are they embarrassed? A couple looks at me like I've just stepped off a UFO.

The teacher talks to us about what goes on in Resource, the help program for kids with various learning disabilities. A few parents complain that they're not kept up on what's happening, and then the meeting is over. We file out, never making eye contact or touching each other, even by accident. We never connect with each other.

Are they all ashamed that they have to go to this room? That their kids aren't brilliant the way this town defines it? Have they learned like Stacy and I that there are different kinds of brilliance besides academic brilliance? Like the brilliance of a wise-cracking kid or a riveting dancer or a budding chef or a teenage rap artist?

Making the Wrong List

BARB

I have just been put on the lay-off list at work. Right before the Thanksgiving holiday. A grim time. Freaking out. We'll have to move out of the area because we can't afford to live here without my salary. Both kids are in high school in Special Ed programs that have taken months, sometimes years of relationship-building to craft together. I make three calls to company vice-presidents I've worked with, just to let them know. The first call back is from Juanita, our most senior African-American vice president. Of all those I've called, I've done the least work with her. Juanita says, "I have one approved opening, and there won't be more for a few months at least. It's yours. It's not for anything you want to do, but it will give you a place to be while you find something you really want to do again."

She literally saves my job and career at the company, because without this safety net — and given my panic and the urgency — I don't know that I would have hung in for the miracles that followed. These miracles include an outright job offer (which I accept) from another vice president, for something I want to do, and intervention by the CEO, who questions my manager as to why I'm on the lay-off list at all.

Meeting Jamal

STACY

On New Year's Eve 2003, our daughter Shawna meets Jamal, a wonderful African-American boy who, like her, is 16. They have an immediate connection, and soon become inseparable, even though he lives in an inner-city neighborhood an hour away.

Jamal spends a lot of time at our suburban home. He becomes a brother to Stephen and a second son to us. Soon, Jamal is hitting Stephen's library; he's never read a book by a Black man before. He says he never even knew that Black men wrote books. We talk non-stop. He has questions, questions, questions. It's so exciting to see and we are falling in love with our new son!

New Life, New Fears

STACY

In May 2004, Shawna and Jamal tell us they are pregnant. They are delighted — we are horrified. He's 17 now, she's still 16. Neither has a high school diploma. Nor a driver's license. They will be babies raising a baby. We let them know what a poor decision we think this is, particularly since Barb and I have talked to our kids about birth control until our voices are hoarse.

When I ask them why they didn't use protection, Shawna responds that they planned this baby. And they are going to have it. And that is that.

We meet Jamal's mom, have dinner together. A vibrant, delightful woman, she is not freaked out about the pregnancy, nor is she overjoyed. Her response to the news was to shout at her son, "You need a J-O-B!" She is very, very funny and we laugh throughout the meal. Soon she feels like an old friend.

Jamal, Barb, and I all go with Shawna to her ultrasound. Our daughter says she already knows it's a boy. We ask, "How do you know?" She says, "I just do. He and I have been talking."

The ultrasound confirms Shawna's intuition. Jamal is beside himself at seeing the images of his son. He gets chills, then nearly faints. His reading immediately shifts from Stephen's books to articles on pregnancy, childbirth, and taking care of a baby.

Come summer, we five head off to Puerto Vallarta. This is Jamal's first time out of state, his first time on an airplane. He's terrified during the plane's ascent, and Barb holds his clammy hand, talks him gently through his fears, calms him down, and helps him to slow his breathing.

We have a great time in Puerto Vallarta. Jamal loves it. We come home to the hotel we're living in while our house is getting renovated, and Jamal continues to be with us.

Life in the War Zone

BARB

Jamal is telling us about his neighborhood, 20 miles from where we live, while Shawna sleeps in the car as we drive home from a day at the beach.

"Mama, I don't wanna go to no more funerals," he says. "I can't stand to see my friends and family lookin' like that ... on a shirt." He explains that when someone dies in his community, they put the person's picture on T-shirts that their loved ones can wear.

That night we meet at the microwave, taking turns making popcorn. "You know, Jamal, you're like a child soldier," I say. "You grew up in a war zone."

"Yeah," he laughs, "two other people told me that too. Kill or be killed. When we was ten or eleven, my cousin and me, we walked to the store to get us some sodas. My mom was workin' the night shift. She don't know we was out. We's walking home and this car comes up, and this guy sticks a shotgun out the window, and his partner jump out and tell us to lie down, and then he get out and hold the shotgun to my neck while the other guy go through our pockets. 'Oh man,' he say, 'you don't got nothing. No weed, no juice, no money, nothing.' 'No man, we ain't got nothing,' I tell him. 'We just getting us a soda.' And he jump back in his car and they drive off. I knowed that night I coulda died. It could happen any time. Just like that. Still could."

Jamal's mom tells us she loves it when he's with us because she knows he's safe. There have been drive-by shootings in their neighborhood lately. Besides, it's not safe even when that's not going on. So Jamal spends most of his time with us, but from time to time goes home because he misses him mom and sisters, and he wants to help his mom.

I think, *How on earth can we send him back to the war zone? But how on earth can we have him move in permanently? We're overextended as it is.*

I tell Stacy about this scene that keeps coming up in my mind. We're on a panel, talking to prospective adoptive parents who are considering cross-racial adoption. I say, "You have no idea how deep and unconscious is your white privilege and how profoundly that shapes the way you think the world is or should be. And, you have no idea how deep and unconscious is the absence of white privilege and how the rhythm and connections of those without it shape their world. You may even raise your children as white, but when they're teenagers, they'll have to choose, and then you will find yourselves in entirely different worlds with no shared language."

Stacy finishes my thought, "Then you step into another universe."

Letter to an Unborn Child

SHAWNA

Shawna has to write a letter to her unborn baby for one of her childrearing classes. She shares it with us and we are struck by the sweetness and the prescience: knowing already that they will be raising each other and learning together.

September 2004
Dear Sweet Baby Boy,

Let's talk about your father. Here are some of his traits:

Just

Active

Money-wise

Adoring

Loving

His name is Jamal and I hope you take some of these qualities. Also your father is very excited. When he heard your heartbeat for the first time, he got the biggest smile on his face. He just lit up with so much happiness and joy.

The first time I felt you move I was lying on my back watching TV. Then I started to feel something weird, and it took me a minute to know it was you. It feels like muscle spasms, and you were kicking for five minutes. I did not think you were going to stop.

My sweet angel, I have so many future hopes for you, but I don't know how to explain them. I want to be the best mother to you, my angel. I think I will because we are learning together. If you help me, I'll help you.

Love,
Your mom

Black on Black

STACY

After two academically successful and emotionally miserable years at the alternative junior high, Stephen has transferred to the mainstream high school. He plays football because he loves it — and with his size and height they're delighted to get him. He does well academically because he has been learning for two years at the alternative school and is beginning to see a future.

Today I'm sitting in the office waiting for a meeting on his Individual Education Plan, the planning document for Resource programs. When asked if I need any help, I mention Stephen's name.

A young African-American man sitting close to me says, "Are you Stephen's mom?"

I say yes.

He says, "I'm the security guard on campus. Yah, I've busted him a couple of times ... he's hanging out with the wrong crowd and he better stop it." He says all this coldly, a mean tone in his voice.

I know about one of these incidents. Stephen — who's now 6-foot-3 — stopped on his way to lunch to chat with some kids on the "path" — the hangout on the way off campus. A couple of the kids were smoking cigarettes. The security guard approached the kids. His story is that Stephen's hand moved toward his pocket, making it look as if Stephen was attempting to hide something. He accused Stephen of trying to hide drugs. Stephen denied it, was made to turn his pockets inside out to prove he wasn't hiding anything, became angry about this, was called "disrespectful" by the security guard, and was marched to the office with the smokers. Stephen protested all the way that he was just headed to lunch and not smoking, but the security guard told the dean of students that Stephen had refused to go to the office. Stephen called me and told me the story.

The dean of students called me to say he was suspending Stephen for two days (the other boys, all white, the smokers, were suspended one day). I told the dean of students Stephen's perspective. The dean said that this did not square with the security guard's story but that he would question some of the smokers independently. He then called me back, said Stephen was right, and said the suspension had been reduced to one day for "bad attitude."

We advise Stephen to stay off that path and to stay away from the security guard, who is now closely watching him.

We ask ourselves what is up with the security guard. Is he watching and waiting in hopes of discovering our Black son doing something wrong, so he can take him in and prove to the white administration that he's on the "white" side? Is it Black internalized racism, where the sadness, rage, and self-hatred a Black person feels is turned outward, directed at those who look like him? Or is it a Black man trying to crush a kid before "the man" can do it? Is it his way of helping?

Is there no relief or safe haven for our son anywhere? The whites are after him but apparently at least one Black man is too. I tell this guard we would appreciate his support and to please let us know if he sees our son being targeted. He doesn't seem to understand what I'm asking. I don't understand where he's coming from.

Homework and High Hopes

BARB

Jamal is finishing his GED in an adult education program near our house and plans to go into law enforcement. He talks about wanting to work undercover. He proudly reports his teacher's constant praises. She's told him several times he's the best reader she's ever had in one of her classes. In the meantime, he has an assignment to complete from the childbirth class through our daughter's hospital. He is to describe all the ways Shawna looks when she is relaxed.

The Terrible Call

STACY

At 3 a.m. Wednesday morning, October 5, 2004, Jamal's mom calls Shawna's cell phone, thinking she's calling me. Shawna, now eight months pregnant, wakes me up and says. "Jamal's mom is crying."

I know instantly what has happened. I don't need her to say it. Barb is in Chicago on a business trip so I grab the phone and all I can understand is, "Jamal's dead, Jamal's dead, Jamal's dead," over and over.

I feel dread and fear take over my body. I don't remember what I say to his mom. I know I try to get some details, but I can't understand most of what she is saying. I do hear her say that Jamal and his good friend, Eric, were shot coming back from the grocery store around 7:30. Jamal was carrying the groceries she sent him to get. Eric is in critical condition, but before he slipped out of consciousness, he said that a guy jumped out of the bushes and just started shooting.

Then her sobbing drowns everything else out. I get off the phone when she says family members have arrived at the house, and I am left with the horrible realization that I have to tell Shawna.

First I call Barb, waking her at 5 a.m. at her hotel in Chicago, where she is scheduled to give a talk at a conference. She is stunned. I tell her I have to tell Shawna.

She says, "I'll stay on the phone and be with you. Bring her in and tell her."

Shawna is up. She knows it's bad. I tell her Mom is on the phone and we have something to tell her.

"Honey, Jamal's been killed."

The sounds that come forth from her mouth are ones I hope I never have to hear again: guttural sounds, hands grasping at the air, voice sobbing, "No, no, no, Mommy, no, no, no ...", over and over again. The wails are so loud, the guy at the front desk of the hotel calls and says there have been complaints about someone shouting. I say it's my daughter, her boyfriend's been murdered. The guy at the desk murmurs his apologies.

Barb talks with Shawna, sobbing with her, herself wailing, "No, no, no! Not our boy. Not this way. Not now ...." The three of us gradually grow hoarse and fall mute, in shock. We let Barb go and I pull my daughter down beside me and rock her until she falls asleep at in the early dawn. Barb cancels her talk and gets the next flight home.

After that there is a whirlwind of activity, a lot of which is a blur. We're very worried that Shawna, now eight months pregnant, will lose their baby. The shock has been terrible.

What If ...
STACY

Shawna came out of her room today with a picture Jamal had told her he wanted on the T-shirts for his funeral when he was killed. When, not if. Shawna told him to hush and didn't want to keep the picture for him, but he talked her into it. We agree to use a different picture instead, one that he also loves, of him and Shawna, with their four hands on her big tummy. One that will honor Jamal's future, not his past. We hug and Shawna sobs. I hold her as tight as I can, with her eight-month belly between us.

My mind keeps going back to the day before the shooting, when I dropped Jamal at the local transit station after taking Shawna to school. I often dropped him at this stop after he had spent time with us.

On this day, for some reason, after I pulled away in my car, I stopped to turn around and look at him. I saw there was absolutely no one around him on the train platform. This struck me as very odd, since it was 8 a.m. on a workday morning. As I watched Jamal slowly shuffle his way to the station door with baggy pants halfway down his butt, like a lot of kids his age, I felt dread. I wanted to shout at him and tell him to come back and get in the car. I didn't, though.

I try not to dwell on this too much, but what *would* have happened if I'd called him back? Would he still be alive? Would our daughter have her partner and her child a daddy?

Every Day I See Black Boys and Men Disappearing

STACY

We've just arrived at the funeral home where Jamal's memorial will be held. We're early, and I have a conversation with the director of the home. He says there are no flowers. There is no money for flowers.

I say, "Let's get some delivered quickly." Then we talk about this tragedy.

He says, "This is my fifth burial of a young Black man this week. At this rate, I don't know if we're going to have any Black boys or Black men left. Between prison and street killings, they are leaving us."

I say, "This is the war at home, the war no one really wants to talk about." As I look at our beautiful boy in his casket, I bend down to kiss him on the forehead. He really does look like he's about to wake up. The whole thing feels surreal.

The police have discovered that Jamal's death was not a gang affair. Indeed our dear boy was not into drugs or gangs, and had no markings of either. The shooter — a childhood friend stoked up and paranoid on three tabs of Ecstasy — mistakenly thought his friends had disrespected his mother and tried killing them all. He killed Jamal on the street, Eric took two bullets but managed to get away before he passed out, and the third friend ran at the first shot and was not hit. The new gun was courtesy of the local drug dealer.

White Gloves Laid on a Casket

BARB

Such a long, painful, rich day, with flashes of joy. There's Jamal's stepbrother, who never knew him but read about his death in the paper and showed up at Jamal's house, looking so much like him, ready to hold Jamal's mom and comfort her. He has Jamal's hands. Stephen and his favorite cousin, Dimitri, are both pallbearers, standing so tall, doing such hard and painful work, carrying their friend's extra-large casket through the church, and later, to the burial ground and into his grave. They carefully fold their white pallbearer gloves and lay them on his lowering casket.

Our daughter, Shawna, is sobbing, "Oh mama, no, no, no, no," as it is time to say our last good-bye to him. But now, for just a moment, she's laughing her infectious laugh with her best friend, who's moved in with us to comfort Shawna and see her through. Thankfully, the members of the Black church where the funeral is held are there testifying, holding, sobbing, laughing, clapping, feeling all there is to feel, and holding all that can never be held any other way, including our family.

My dear friend Nancy has printed out on our big company printer a huge canvas picture of Shawna and Jamal, beaming, with their hands folded over her swollen belly. This image is the centerpiece of the service and the burial, the photo we use on Jamal's memorial T-shirts, and the pride of Jamal's mom. It is her greatest comfort and will have pride of place in her living room for years to come.

I stand up to read at the funeral, suddenly terrified I will be interpreted by this mostly Black congregation (our white friends and family are the only white people present) as some kind of white honky disrespecting this beloved boy. I have before me what I have written on the plane home, writing being — as it often is for me — the only way I can stop crying. Ah well, it is what it is. I begin reading.

In fact, after three lines I am no longer just reading. I am engaged in some kind of magical mystical call and response rap, a co-creation swelling with and swallowing, for just a moment, our overwhelming sorrow, embracing us all in some kind of huge soft spirit. Here are my words and in italics are the words I remember the congregation crying out, thereby transforming my offering to Jamal into the most powerful spiritual experience of my life.

Dear dear boy
We thank God for our time
With you
Yes God, yes we do...
Dear gentle soul...
Your soft chuckle
Your big laugh
Yeah baby, that's him, you got it!
Sitting on the stoop
Together, talking about life,
You jump up,
"Hey, Mama
Wanna hand up?
Here, Mama,
Wanna hand up?"
Yeah, that be Jamal
Singin' in the back seat
With your CDs
Oh yeah, CDs
A song only you can hear.

We hear your voice,
Yes we do, we do
Jamal,
We hear you baby,
We hear you now and forever...
Yes baby, now, fuhevah
Hey, Mama,
Ima get me that GED
Take the test in February...
It's goin' real good, Mama
So good, oh so good mama
She say, the teacher she say
I'm the best reader she ever had
Yes he is, he is...
Damn...
I read real good, mama ...
Hey, Mama,
Ima be a daddy to my son
Oh yeah, mama, a daddy
Teach him things
I don' want my baby
Growin' up with no daddy ...
No, no more no daddy
Dear God,
In this hour, this day, this lifetime
Of our need.
God, please be with us.
Oh yeah God, be here, hear us
And help us find the ways
To stop this killing of our sons,

Stop the killin', stop the killin'
Brothers, lovers, partners,
Stop the killin'
Our sons,
Our hopes, our dreams, our future,
Yes our future, our future
Our sons.
Our sons.
Yeah baby, thassit, thassit. Amen, Amen, Amen.

Shawna goes to the front to read her letter to their unborn child. She cannot make it through because she cannot stop quietly crying. She is joined by Jamal's mother, who holds her as she finishes her reading.

Then Stacy sings a Greek lament in the minor chords of all Greek laments, a wailing she keens for Jamal. Her voice, her words both tear and soothe our hearts.

Jamal William Johnson,
Gentle spirit, tender soul
That smile you smiled so sweetly
Soothed and warmed the hearts of all
Jamal William Johnson,
Your baby boy is on his way
He will have you in him
He will know you every day
Shawna and this village,
We'll love that child with all our might
He's the baby, Jamal,
Who brings us hope, who brings us light

We hear you our dear Jamal
You are telling us you're fine
You say remember I'm right here with you
And I'll meet you when it's your time
Jamal, you now know
The deepest peace and love
You're with the ones who've gone before
Wrapped in the arms of God
Jamal William Johnson,
We pledge our deepest vow
We will not give in to hatred
We'll bring the peace somehow
The peace you'd want, sweet Jamal,
For all you know and love
The peace we need across our world
A peace to bless your son
Jamal William Johnson,
Your journey does not end
We say good-bye only for now
Until we meet again
Until we meet again
Hallelujah
Hallelujah
Hallelujah
Amen
Amen
Amen

As the funeral draws to a close, everyone sobs
and holds on to each other. This is no video game or
action movie where people get up after they're shot.

This is the end. Forever. Of this beautiful boy and his modest and impossible dreams.

It's Not Just a Black Problem
STACY

The funeral is over. We have no words to express our sadness and grief. Jamal was one of the sweetest, kindest, most loving people we have ever known. His heart was open, his spirit generous and spacious. He loved our daughter very much and she deeply loved him. Barb and I were so grateful that Shawna had found such a wonderful young man.

The violent, senseless death of this beautiful young man is only one of many deaths like this happening all over our country. In certain inner cities, some say, it is to be expected. But these aren't the only places it's happening. Last week, an 18-year-old was shot to death in the town next to ours, a nice, "safe," suburban community. A friend visiting Shawna tells us today she has lost four friends and two family members, all under 20, all in this past year, all dead from gunfire just a few miles from our town. This young woman is 18, and she tells us this matter-of-factly.

We know this is not just a "Black problem" or a "Mexican problem." We have only to recall the Columbine massacre to know that.

How as a country, as communities, as individuals do we address these devastating issues? War is not occurring just in Iraq. War is happening right here on our soil. On our doorstep. Our young people are suffering, and they are killing each other. There are no foreign terrorists doing this. We have allowed the social, political, and economic conditions in our own country to get to a place where many of our young people reach a place of such desperation that they are harming themselves and each other in one way or another. Drugs, alcohol, guns. We can deny it and hide, saying these are just "thugs," "crazy kids," "young criminals." We can say, "Oh for heaven's sake, this is America! All anyone has to do is pull themselves up by their bootstraps and get on with it."

Or we can begin to ask ourselves the question, *What is really going on here? What is our response-ability in the matter?*

As a nation, we recognize the devastation of 9/11. We are determined to find terrorists "wherever they may be," expending thousands of lives and billions of dollars doing so. We think that will make us safe. What about Jesus' words: "First take the log out of your own eye, and then you will see clearly to take out the speck that is in your brother's eye." Every major faith has some equivalent to this spiritual axiom.

Do we understand that Jamal lived in a war zone? Can we grasp the paradox that on some level he was expecting to die even as he was joyfully preparing for his son to be born? Do we get that he wasn't a bad kid, not even a gang member, or a thug, and that he didn't have it coming? Do we recognize that there are many war zones in the U.S., even though we may not ourselves live in one? Are we awake to the need to pay attention to what's going on right in front of us, in addition to what's going on in the rest of the world? Can we bear to give up the illusion that we are safe, and that life, in fact, doesn't guarantee us safety? Are we willing to ask the question, why are so many of our young people in despair, and not engage in blame or recrimination?

Can we face the fact that just like in Iraq and other places in the world, we have places in this country that are Third World, that are experiencing genocide, and where people are taking up arms either to protect themselves or with intent to harm others? Do we sense that the borders, fences, and nice neighborhoods we erect don't really protect us from anything except the truth? Can we entertain the idea that our trying to bring democracy and freedom to the world may strike others in the world as arrogant (a "log in our eye") and hypocritical, given what's happening on our own domestic front?

Most importantly, can we actually have dialogue around any of this, given our emotions and disagreements? And not just dialogue with those we like or love, but dialogue with those who drive us crazy, who get on our last nerve, whose views are diametrically opposed to our own, whose positions we consider fundamentalist and beyond reach?

I had a really good conversation with some of my cousins not too long ago. We grew up together and love one another very much. During our conversation, we disagreed (forcefully!) in the area of politics. But after a while, we did seem to agree on some basic things, and one of them is that we feel there is enough collective intelligence and heart in this world — and specifically in this country — to compassionately and effectively address many of the issues that are tearing us apart.

Down

BARB

Our daughter lies in bed mute. She can't talk about what's happened, how she feels or even what she wants to eat. She has no more joy in the coming baby, her dream project with Jamal, her future. We try to tempt her with her favorite foods. We remove the large piece of broken glass she's put by the side of her bed.

Stacy and I are very worried and are also mute with grief. We coax Shawna to eat by fixing her favorite fried chicken, forgetting it was Jamal's signature dish, remembering with the food in front of us all the times he fixed it for the whole family as we laughed and talked about the future.

As I toss out the chicken, I imagine I'm making a food offering to the all-powerful Grim Reaper who can strike any time, taking the life of any child any time, relentlessly crushing the hope and joy of those who remain. *Please, please, please,* I pray. *Give us a break: Pass us over for a while and leave us alone.*

Stacy's and my conversations are purely logistical: Who can watch our daughter when we're both at work? Is there any way to get the doctor Shawna wants to deliver her baby or must we accept the rotation crapshoot and get someone she's never met? (To jump ahead: There isn't, we get the crapshoot, the doctor is a nightmare autocrat causing such pain and hardship for our daughter that our doula refuses to work with him ever again.) What to do about the latest attack on our son, this time by the dean of students? Isn't it your turn to clean up the kitchen — I did it last time! Can't you pick up the package at FedEx? It's probably something you ordered!

Stacy's online ordering picks up; it's the one way she can find some pleasure. Presents in the mail make the day a little easier. Her guilt grows: We can't afford this way out. I take increasingly frequent breaks by stepping outside the house for a cigarette, a big problem since I now have emphysema. Friends say, "Don't you realize you're killing yourself?" and I feel a grim satisfaction that I have taken the power into my own hands for exiting this life sooner than later. I cannot bear one more thing: losing another child, even dealing with the next experience of overkill with our son by either the vigilantes, the school or the police.

The Grim Reaper stalks us, robbing us of light and hope. We seem to be living inside a tunnel, buried underground, gray, gray, gray.

Jamal's mother, stepfather and little sister come over and spend the weekend, weekend after weekend. We sit out in the backyard with a carton of cigarettes and a quart of vodka, smoking out our rage, drinking ourselves into tears, remembering, remembering. Often, it seems Jamal's just coming around the corner. Often, he's come to one of us in a dream and given us a message. We hang out in his favorite places in the house, in the yard, around the neighborhood. We recall conversations. We hear of his childhood. We share dozens of pictures between us of this beautiful boy. Remembering, remembering.

Shawna drifts through these gatherings, nibbling, saying a word, contributing a picture or a story, and sometimes even giving us all the hint of a smile.

Up: Hope Returns

STACY

Our daughter starts her contractions and we go to the hospital. It will be a 44-hour labor, agonizingly slow. She doesn't want an epidural and she doesn't want a Caesarean. She wants a natural birth.

But that's not the way it goes and our doctor is our nightmare, a throwback to the fifties when the doctor was God. With no warning, he breaks her water. With no warning, he gets ready to give her a shot to prepare her for surgery, a shot that we haven't even discussed and that Shawna doesn't want.

Shawna ends up having two epidurals and a Caesarean. Only one of us moms can go into the delivery room. Barb goes in and I wait. In a matter of minutes, the nurse comes out and hands me the baby, our gorgeous little grandson, and he and I go off to the nursery. I am there for his first bath and the medicating of his eyes. It is wonderful to be there, and I'm so grateful that he's healthy.

Shawna names her son Jamal, after his daddy. From the moment little Jamal arrives, hope returns. At first (and even years later), it is sometimes bittersweet. You gasp at the child's beauty and then imagine in a heartbeat it's gone.

This baby is so sweet. Our healing slowly begins. Shawna struggles. It is hard to see this little one, who looks like his daddy, and not see all the broken dreams and feel the brutal reality that anything could happen any time with *this* Jamal, or with anyone else we love.

Sometimes at night, baby Jamal looks to the ceiling and just stares. His daddy was a football player, and we all believe he's looking at Daddy ... who is looking down at him. He wakes up laughing, every morning, refreshed. We think he and his daddy play angel football at night while the rest of us sleep.

One thing for sure, Baby Jamal moves like his daddy. At eight months he can throw a ball from his high chair. At 10 months he takes his first three steps. Ten minutes later, he pivots and then runs.

Barb and I find ourselves incredibly grateful for the pregnancy, which we had thought was the biggest mistake ever. For sure this baby is keeping his other grandmother on the planet, so lost in grief is she. But she can see her boy in his son and now, together with Shawna and Barb and me, she must stick around and help raise this baby.

Teen pregnancy in Black and Brown communities takes on new meaning for Barb and me. We see it not only as the mistake most of our Black and white professional friends think it is, but also as a desperate attempt by a family bloodline to ensure that a family goes on, given that so many of the boys are dead or in prison before they can start families. The desperate plea of one of Shawna's girlfriends to Barb to help her see if she can get sperm from her boyfriend who's just been killed, so she can give his family a baby, reinforces our unorthodox perception.

Our Little Sunflower
STACY

My Zen teacher, Marie, invites me to bring baby Jamal to the Zen temple for a blessing. I love this teacher and our Zen practice, and I realize how much it would mean to me for her to bless him.

When I arrive, Marie opens the door and reaches out her arms. I put Jamal into them. I join the other students and sit on my meditation cushion. Marie kisses the baby's head and speaks her blessing. At the end of the little ceremony, she turns Jamal so he faces all of us and says, "I name this child Sunflower."

I get goose bumps. This is an absolutely perfect name for this sweet, sunny child.

I spend the rest of the service gently rocking Jamal. "Baby Sunflower."

The Collapse of an Alpha Female
STACY

A year and a half after Jamal gets the Zen version of a christening, Barb receives a phone call at work from my Zen teacher. Marie tells Barb that she has just gotten a call from me to say goodbye. In that call, I reminded Marie that I have been struggling with depression for years and told her I had decided I didn't want to be here anymore. I was going to commit suicide.

Marie tells Barb she has convinced me to drive the hour and a half to Marie's home before I do anything, in order to say good-bye in person. Then, although she has not told me about this plan, Marie and her husband will drive me back to a hospital near our home. Barb agrees to meet my teacher, her husband and me at the hospital.

Once I'm admitted, hospital personnel contact my psychotherapist. She tells them, "Don't let her fool you. She presents well and it will seem she's fine. She's not."

Barb arrives, deeply shaken. In shock, I'm admitted to the closed unit and put on suicide watch.

Later that day, as Barb and I are sitting on a couch waiting to see a doctor, a young African-American man comes out of a room and sits at a table near us. He seems very nice but quite withdrawn. Barb and I continue to talk quietly about what's happened and the logistics to be faced, when suddenly the young man stands up, walks over to where we are, and begins ranting about how our relationship is the reason I am sick and in the hospital, that this is God's revenge for our sin. Then he goes back to his table.

Barb jumps up, strides to the nurses' station and asks for help. Then she requests — and finally demands — that I be moved to another unit. While Barb's asking for help, I walk over to the young man and tell him I didn't need to hear his crap and I never want to hear it from him again. Not my finest moment ....

The nurse, very anxious now, tells me to stop and go sit down. I'm having a hard time controlling my anger. She repeats, "Go sit down and I'll come over and explain something."

It turns out this young man is suffering from paranoid delusional thinking and religious ideation, meaning that he sees his own persecution in religious terms, and in our case is projecting it onto us. When I find out his room is right across from mine, I demand a move, which Barb has already gotten going. Having worked my way through school as a nurse's aide on psychiatric units, I understand where this young man is at and the harm he's capable of. What if he loses it in the night and decides to kill me because God told him to? If I am going to die, I want it to be by my own hand, not his.

I find it ironic that this incident kicks off my hospitalization. Isn't there anywhere on the planet I can get away from this kind of assault?

The rest of my stay is beneficial. I sleep, I relax. I have time to reflect on my life, my utter loss of joy in it, the unrelenting pressure of kids and jobs and racism and sexism and homophobia. I have time to visit with the friends who come by.

It is hard to explain to them what happened to me. Several share their fears that it could happen to them, since their lives have similar pressures. I say I suddenly couldn't take any of it any more. I felt saturated, overwhelmed, full of despair, empty of joy or peace.

I am an Alpha female: strong, self-confident, a leader. But Alphas, like all people, need nurturance, time, space, sleep, and pleasure in their lives. I had thought I would be able to handle everything that had been thrown our way without worrying about those things. I didn't realize that when the gas tank gets empty, you need to refill it. I didn't realize that applied to me, too. I had lived on fumes for a long, long time before this hit.

I am strong, but not superhuman. I needed a wake-up call. I got one.

Further Down

BARB

I am angry and terrified. Stacy and I were holding it all together and now she's checked out. I feel like I have four children: our two kids, the baby and now her. I'm enraged that she's deserted me and grateful beyond all words that she didn't go all the way, as the partner of a dear friend did just the week before, jumping from their penthouse apartment to her death. The fact that my friend's partner is the first lesbian provost of a huge university offers no immunity. In fact, some of the couple's friends believe that the homophobia she's encountered in the provost job is just one more thing that pushed her out the window.

I may be angry, but my anger pales in comparison to my dear friend's guilt and grief after losing her partner altogether.

Stacy's doctor queries me intently about how it's going, leaves the conference room, then returns to say that she and her staff believe I, too, should be hospitalized. I can't imagine how they have come up with this or how it could remotely occur. I reassure them I'm okay, work is going fine, and with their help we're keeping the family on track.

I'm on automatic, going through the paces, getting through one day and one long night at a time.

Up: The T-Shirt Lectures
— and This Book

BARB

Work is saving me. I go to meetings, respond to a
few hundred emails a day, and as Stacy improves, I
resume travel. I introduce one change into my
normal routine. Everywhere I go, I reframe things so
that I can talk about Jamal. This innovation begins
in my cubicle, with every friend who stops by. It
continues into formal settings. I am to speak at a
major local university a few weeks after the funeral.
The professor calls to say she's prepared to cancel.
"Surely you want some more time off after the death
of your son-in-law?" I tell her I need to come to her
class. I need to talk.

I am to speak on social innovation, as it's played
out at my company and as I've written about it in my
book *Soul in the Computer*, which the class has been
assigned to read. But instead of talking about social
innovation at my company, which I remind them
they've already read about, I challenge this bright
young group to tackle the biggest social innovation
challenge in our country: how to reverse the
systematic destruction of Black youth. I tell them
Jamal's story, I show pictures of his funeral T-shirt.
I tell them what I believe: that if they wanted to, this
very class could map out the blueprint for leading
this country forward into justice and liberty for all. I
challenge them to complete the promise of the
American Revolution. That is the supreme social
innovation of which they are capable, and all the

tools I've discussed in my previous book should be applied to this challenge.

The students come up and hug me at the end of the "lecture." Several confide that my story has changed their life. The professor later reports to me that some of them have changed their projects to contribute towards what they are calling the big blueprint for reversing the destruction of Black youth.

And Stacy climbs out of the pit of despair, slowly but surely. She passes me on her way up. Thank God she is now stepping up again to share the burden of our lives. She is upbeat and back in touch with her dreams of doing something in film. Soon she has a walk-on part in a new movie by an African friend who came back into our lives after the death of Jamal.

I can now travel and I agree to speak to an engineering class at a prestigious women's college back East. Once again, I reframe the assignment. I challenge them to the greatest engineering challenge of our time: engineering this country into a future beyond the pernicious and systemic racism that is killing off Black youth. Once again, I show a picture of the funeral T-shirt, which to me has become the emblem of truth and of our country's shame, the starting point for anything beyond.

At the end of this "lecture," one of the few African-American students in the class, who has waited to be last in line to talk with me, takes me aside and whispers, "I'm so glad you talked about Jamal and the T-shirt. I come from a neighborhood like his. No one at this school knows anything about me." This is so sad to me — this school prides itself on building community among young women, creating an environment where their deepest hopes and dreams can be shared and flourish. This young woman continues, "The thing is, in my school we don't do T-shirts. Every year, on the longest wall of the school, we paint the faces and death-dates of every student killed that year. We make a memorial to the friends we lose. Every year we paint over the wall and start again. That wall is just layers and layers of dead kids...."

I am speechless and my eyes and heart are full of tears. We hug each other as the instructor looks nervously on, no doubt wondering what on earth is happening. The student walks me out to the patio and continues to talk while I take a cigarette break.

I am coming to realize that I can keep going if I can keep giving words to my anguish and my questions. But I can't turn everything into a T-shirt lecture.

I start writing this book.

The Passing of a Good Man
STACY

After a very painful year-long battle with cancer, my dad dies. We had grown so close after he chose to speak out at our 25th anniversary party. His actions deeply affected my relationship with him. I was so grateful that we had come to a place of peace and understanding.

My dad showed me that it's never too late to change, never too late to experience forgiveness and reconciliation — and that you never know when and how this kind of change can happen. You can be surprised and moved in unimaginable ways if you keep your heart open to the possibilities.

Derision Where Praise Is Due

BARB

I actually feel sorry for Bill O'Reilly. The Fox News Channel host recently went to dinner at a famous Harlem restaurant with civil rights activist Al Sharpton, and is being ridiculed and attacked now because he shared his experience with his radio audience. He told them, with wonder, that African-American restaurants — just like white ones — are full of families, the food is just as good, the tables as clean.[11] As a result, O'Reilly is derided by liberal media — the media we listen to and watch — for his ignorance, for not already knowing this. More

---

[11] According to the transcript of the radio show, O'Reilly said, "I couldn't get over the fact that there was no difference between Sylvia's restaurant and any other restaurant in New York City. I mean, it was exactly the same, even though it's run by Blacks, primarily Black patronship." Later, during an interview, he added, "There wasn't one person in Sylvia's who was screaming, 'M-fer, I want more iced tea ...' It was like going into an Italian restaurant in an all-white suburb in the sense of people were sitting there, and they were ordering and having fun. And there wasn't any kind of craziness at all."

informed and superior-feeling commentators are having a field day that he could be so clueless in this day and age.

Despite the fact that I can't stand O'Reilly's network, his show, or his views, I feel such sadness, even grief, that we are treating him this way. What if we celebrated this "clueless" white guy for going to an African-American restaurant in the first place, in spite of his obvious misgivings and ignorance? What if we thanked him for his honesty in sharing his experience?

Instead of a pariah, O'Reilly could be a bridge for the millions of others who haven't got a clue, a bridge from separateness into our common humanity. The celebration could become reassurance to everyone that it's good to take a risk, to reach out, to go deeper in this quest to see what we have in common. Instead, the derision just proves to people that it's too risky to reach across the divide, that there are too many minefields in the terrain, that you will, somehow, be blown up if you try cross into new territory.

Living in Both Cultures
STACY

Over the years, we've gotten the question, "Do you think it's hard on your kids that they don't belong in either the white culture or the Black culture?"

That question used to make me cringe inside. My worst fear is that we've done something to harm our children.

And there is some truth to the fact that it can be very difficult straddling two cultures.

But what we actually see says something different. Rather than seeing themselves without a culture, they feel they have two cultures. Among their Black friends, they might speak Ebonics, blast rap music, and generally fit in with whatever's happening. Around white people (mostly adults), they can change to the "King's English," tone down, and, once again, fit in. Then again, their white friends are often trying to be Black, so that's not necessarily a conflict!

I am bicultural. I grew up Greek, and in my father's eyes, there were Greeks and whites. The Greek culture has its own rules for belonging, and I had to learn those rules as well as the rules of the majority culture. It didn't hurt me. It helped. And though I realize being Greek is not the same as being Black in terms of the enculturation process, both my kids and I have had to learn to be culturally competent in two very different cultures. And there's nothing like direct experience to speed the learning.

Barb always reminds me of the Southern saying, "What don't kill is fattenin'."

I guess that means all four of us have gotten plenty fat.

But What Do You Stand Up *For?*

BARB

I am the speaker at a virtual conference of 160 of our company's employees around the world, all meeting by dialing in to a conference-call number. We are discussing globalization and its impact at all levels and how we can stand up for improving things. I mention a good thing about globalization: We come to better grasp where the U.S. stands in the global community on critical issues. I give as an example the recent vote on a U.N. resolution calling for the abolition of life imprisonment without the possibility of parole for children and young teenagers. The vote was 185 to 1, with the U.S. being the lone dissenter.

One of the listeners writes in later, calling me to task. "How can you applaud the courage to stand up for what you believe in, but at the same time put down the U.S. for doing just that?"

On the one hand I want to scream at how clueless this remark is. On the other, I am so grateful to this anonymous employee that he is staying in the conversation with me and asking a question that's really on his mind.

I reply that it's not just the fact of standing up or forming partnerships with others that matters, it's what we are we standing up *for*. If the U.S. stood up for building the best juvenile rehabilitation programs in the world, that is a "standing up" I would applaud because of what the standing up was for.

It's Not Fair

STACY

Shawna, now 20, calls me to say that she just got stopped by the police in the wealthy, old-money city adjacent to ours. She was driving with baby Jamal, now

2½, when she merged onto a freeway and the guy behind her (a white man) blew his top. He flipped her the bird, then sidled up to the right side of her car so closely, the cars nearly touched. It felt like he was trying to run her off the road. Both Shawna and the man exited the freeway. Shawna, angry and very shaken, rolled down the passenger window and grabbed the top of her perfume bottle. She wanted to throw it at him. But she changed her mind, opened her driver's side window, and tossed the perfume cap out that side. She called the police and they took a report of the "he said/she said" variety. No blame was assigned.

About two weeks later, Shawna gets a notice from the man's insurance company, claiming that she threw a rock at his car and damaged it. Outraged, I call our insurance company and they tell me to get a copy of the police report. The police won't give us one, however, because there is a warrant out for Shawna's arrest!

According to the police, the D.A. has decided to press charges. We appear before the judge and bail is set at $5,000 — the tipping point. This means Shawna will have to appear several times in court. I call Tom, our wonderful attorney. He walks me through the process of getting a bail bondsperson to post bail.

While talking to our attorney, I say, "This feels like a racist, bogus charge."

He says. "Absolutely. The police know that their mandate is to keep that city 'clean and white.' It's been going on for a long, long time."

I talk with Shawna, and her response is, "Why? It's not fair!"

Our attorney says, "Who's talking about fair? This has nothing to do with fairness."

I feel my blood boil. First, our daughter and grandson are assaulted on the road and could have been seriously injured or killed. Then this man, who clearly was under the influence of road rage, says his car is damaged. And it's our daughter who has been nailed by the police. Oh yes, and the police never saw the so-called damage.

The bail bondsman is Latino and very helpful. He speaks of his own experiences of being targeted for "driving while brown." He says this charge is so silly, it's unbelievable it could have come so far.

The easiest thing now would be to jump through the hoops, get Shawna cleared, and forget about it. But I'm not sure if that's what we'll do. We're seriously thinking about suing this man, who has caused needless worry and anxiety for a young woman who is going to community college, working part-time, and raising her son as a single mom.

We're also considering suing the police department for racist behavior. Just because they've been operating this way for many years doesn't mean they should be able to continue to do so. But before we can get any further with this situation, we have to get on with the next outrage.

Here We Go Again

BARB

It's 10 p.m. and I am picking up Stephen, now 17, on the kids' main drag in our town. He's not there and a police car has just sped past. I'm worried sick. I call Stephen on his cell. "Where are you?"

"Coming in just a few minutes," he says.

I wait in the dark for 15 minutes, a white woman safely parked in a nice safe white town, scared to death for my Black son. Finally he saunters up, hops in the car, and flips on the music as we head home. When we get back, we've gotten a call from Tish, the mother of one of the two boys Stephen was with tonight. She says the police stopped the three boys (two African-Americans and one Mexican) for jaywalking. They were all frisked and issued citations. This is not a city that cites people for jaywalking. It just doesn't happen. Except if you're Black or Mexican.

"Why didn't you tell me what happened?" I ask Stephen.

"Mom, it doesn't concern you. It happens every day. They just wait for us." He goes on to say that the white cop, while writing out the citations, almost got hit by a driver doing an illegal U-turn. The driver was not cited. The driver was white.

"You have no idea what my life is like," Stephen adds.

Tish, the African-American mom, is enraged. She's about to file a complaint about another incident in which the police stopped her other son, made the kids get out of the car, and searched it, even taking the seats out. She says the police have parked in front of their house every day for 10 days. And she's had to wait three months for an appointment to discuss this incident with them.

I tell her Stacy went down to the police station the last time our son was stopped. He was charged with driving without a license. The knucklehead — of course you have to have a license! We took away his keys and disabled the car. As usual, when our kids screw up we had double work: take on the kid, then take on the system.

Stacy wants to find out why Stephen was stopped in the first place. According to the officer, his tail light was out. This is strange, because we had his car completely checked out two days earlier. Stacy calls the people that towed away Stephen's car and asks them to check the tail lights. Both are working. She calls the police back. They will not discuss this unless she comes down in person.

Stacy takes a day off work to go down. She asks to see the police report. There is no mention of a tail light.

"Well," says the officer on duty, "the patrolman just didn't write it down."

"Well," Stacy says, "it's also not broken. Let me talk to your supervisor."

The supervisor comes out.

Stacy says, "Look, this is a case of stopping my son for the crime of Driving While Black. We expect you to pay for the car's towing and storage, have the car returned to our home, and cease harassing our son."

The supervisor agrees it shouldn't have happened and agrees to get the car out of hock and return it to us at the city's expense.

Now Stephen tells us he's getting harassed several times a week, sometimes every day. I wake up on Saturday crying that my son and I live in two different towns, two different countries, two different worlds.

Of course my son is not perfect. Few 17-year-old boys are. But he's getting in far more trouble far more often than he deserves. Talk about a paper trail. It's frightening.

I tell Stephen we have to get him out of our town as soon as possible. He must finish high school so we can send him to college in Atlanta, where there are at least more Blacks and some safe neighborhoods, or in Mexico, where the brown people don't have such a thing about Black people. He agrees this is the right plan.

We're the Lucky Ones

STACY

Throughout the years, we have heard, "Wow, these kids are so lucky to have you." We feel taken aback, although we appreciate the sentiment. The truth is, we are the lucky ones. We feel grateful and privileged to have this amazing opportunity. Because of these kids, we have been taken in by so many people in the Black community, and have a chance to be part of the lives of so many wonderful people.

No one gets out of this life unscathed. Being awake to that suffering is the way to joy, not necessarily happiness. Joy, we've found, is present in every condition we face.

Basically all that means is that if we are able to stay fully in the moment, we find ultimate fulfillment. In our lives as a family, we certainly have not been able to experience that joy all the time. But when we do, when we can open our hearts to these kids, to the communities in which we live, to the world, there is peace even when there is pain. Peace and pain sit together, within us. There is a line out of a Buddhist chant that says, "No old age and death, and no end to old age and death." Practicing daily with this kind of duality, contradiction, mystery, is what brings us to acceptance of life as it is, and to the right actions we need to take.

When we don't practice — when we don't sit daily on a meditation cushion for at least a half hour, watching what comes up in our minds as we hold these paradoxes — there is often confusion, overwhelm, and resistance. Especially when we are facing difficult experiences in life. When we do practice, an intuitive "rightness" happens. We know what to do and how to do it.

This is not a mere intellectual exercise. It's a way of life. And because we are human, we forget to do the things we know work, like meditation practice. We forget a lot. And then we remember again. I had not sat in meditation for months before I went into the hospital. I now do so, because my life depends on it.

A Prize Idiot

BARB

I am reading in the morning paper that James D. Watson, the scientist who shared a Nobel Prize for discovering the structure of DNA and a former director of the Human Genome Project, has opened his mouth again and delighted racists around the world. Watson has declared that the future of Africa is gloomy because it's full of Black people and they are genetically inferior.[12]

I do not let myself feel outrage and despair that Watson is at it again. He has never stopped on this train of thought. White people who are appalled or seek to appear that way force him to apologize every time. And then he just does it again.

He's consistent in his hatred of people different from himself, too. Ten years ago he told a British newspaper that a woman should have a right to abort her unborn child if science could determine the child would be homosexual.

Rescuing and Control?

BARB

I head off to my Al-Anon meeting, the 12-step program I've been going to since 1981 to remember my own needs. The topic is rescuing and control: how we rescue people in order to control situations

---

[12] Watson was quoted in London's *Sunday Times* as saying he was "inherently gloomy about the prospect of Africa" because "all our social policies are based on the fact that their intelligence is the same as ours — whereas all the testing says not really." He added that while it was natural to believe all humans are equal in intelligence, "people who have to deal with Black employees find this is not true."

and how fruitless and exhausting the effort is. There's lots of good sharing, and like many of the parents there, I'm thinking about ways I can back off of rescuing my kids and coworkers so that they can better learn cause and effect, and the consequences of their actions.

But then I find myself saying to the group, "I get it about rescue and control and the illness that can be. What I don't get is where my responsibility fits in." I talk about the night with my son and the blatantly racist jaywalking citation, and how exhausted I am and how much I don't want to go down to the police station and file my umpteenth complaint and listen to all their excuses one more time. I think about how I shortly have to pack up and fly across the country to be on a panel, even though I'm not over my bronchitis and I have way too much work to do, and Stacy and I haven't budgeted the time away from the family for me to go to this conference.

I start crying about how exhausted I am, but I don't see how I can give up responsibility because there are too few people at work on fixing these systems and if those who are working on them give up, then we'll slide even further back. I look into the faces of many caring women who look like me, I am given many hugs, and I'm told again and again that I have to take care of myself and that the rest will have to wait.

I hear them but I still don't get it. How can I rest? How can battling what my son's facing wait? I remain confused on this point. Then the only Black woman in the meeting comes up to me and puts her arms around me in a deep warm hug. Afterwards, she steps back and with tears in her eyes says, "Yes, I know what you mean. I'm confused too. Bless you, my sister."

PART IV:
FIRST STEPS INTO ADULTHOOD

Resilience Rules

STACY

Shawna, now 20, is attending a junior college with the goal of opening a center for unwed teen mothers. She's clear that she has much to offer and we totally agree. Shawna has emerged from her teens into a responsible adult and a loving mom. It's truly a miracle to behold.

Our little grandson, Jamal, is the love of our lives. Curious, verbal, active, and bright, he is such an awesome incarnation of both his parents. We are typical doting grandparents — I suspect we drive others crazy with our myriad of little Jamal stories and our latest pictures.

Stephen has turned 18 and is pursing the flair for cooking he's shown since he could stand on a chair at the stove. During his junior year in high school, he did an apprenticeship program for school credit at a restaurant in our town owned by Wolfgang Puck. He got an A and 5 credits. He's good — really good. And he has a passion for it.

Because the rest of the high school experience bored Stephen deeply and he was being targeted by several staff members (although he also had advocates who risked their jobs to defend him), he decides he will study for the GED rather than do his senior year. We think this is a great idea. He leaves to check out the Cordon Bleu culinary school in London. Amazing. He calls two days later to say the school is okay, but he doesn't like the city. It's racist. We ask him for an example.

He says, "Everybody coming toward me on the sidewalk crosses to the other side of the street. But don't worry about it. I called Dimitri (his Greek cousin) and he said to just stay in my room when I'm not looking at the school, so that's what I'm doing."

God, one of the most fabulous cities in the world, and all he's seeing of it are the walls of a third-rate (a.k.a. affordable) hotel room.

We'll find a school that works in a city better than our own and better than London. We hope.

And Now, 2008 Elections

STACY

It's amazing that we stand at the crossroads of a primary where a woman and a Black man are vying for the Democratic presidential nomination. Maybe this will be a time when content and issues will trump personality and character assassination. Maybe this moment signals an era of compassion and humility rather than egotism and arrogance. Maybe whoever assumes this role will actually be able to address the issues of our country that for so long have gone neglected. Maybe.

Our slice of life, our microcosm, is reflective of the macrocosm, the greater whole. Our experiences, including the suffering, parallel the suffering in this country. The "change" being called for is as much on the individual level as it is on the macro level.

For us, the change called for is for every person to see his or her part in the continuation and ending of prejudice, of all the "isms." Seeing begins with a courageous decision to notice one's own thoughts and actions. It means being willing to see our own racism, homophobia, or anything that separates us from others.

As far as we can tell, no one is exempt. If we start with the assumption that everyone has some degree of bias, accompanied by words and actions, we can bypass the "who is and who isn't" game and get on with noticing, acknowledging, intending, committing, and changing.

Cause for Joy

BARB

It's May 15, 2008, and we are astounded — and thrilled — to learn that the California Supreme Court has voted 4-3 that the state law preventing same-sex couples from marrying is unconstitutional. The chief justice of the Republican-dominated court, Ronald M. George, writes, "In view of the substance and significance of the fundamental constitutional right to form a family relationship, the California Constitution properly must be interpreted to guarantee this basic civil right to all Californians, whether gay or heterosexual, and to same-sex couples as well as to opposite-sex couples.

"Our state now recognizes that an individual's capacity to establish a loving and long-term committed relationship with another person and responsibly to care for and raise children does not depend upon the individual's sexual orientation." He adds, "An individual's sexual orientation — like a person's race or gender — does not constitute a legitimate basis upon which to deny or withhold legal rights."

Just Enough Time to Grab a Quick ... Wedding

BARB

After 33 years together, Stacy and I are getting legally married. At first, I have no great hopes that we'll pull it off before the November election, when California voters get to decide whether we should be allowed to be married. To start with, we have to find my divorce decree from way back when (we end up having to send for a copy). Next we have to get down to the courthouse to file the paperwork. Sounds simple, but when do we have time?

Then one day when we are getting our haircuts, one of the stylists points out that we're in the county seat and we just "have to!" get married. We decide to pop over to the courthouse and see how far we can get with the process. That's when the Miracle of the Straight People begins.

First is Regina, the clerk. We get to her position at the counter before we've even filled out the forms, imagining we'd never get this far. Instead of sending us to the back of the line, as she has every right to do, she whispers that she'll just take her break now and let us stand at her counter till we get them filled in.

Stacy asks if there is any chance we can get into the chapel today. No, Regina says, it's completely booked. Stacy explains how hard it is for us to get down to the courthouse — we live a ways away and we have way too much going on, work- and family-wise. Regina finds a cancellation, provided we raced downstairs to the chapel immediately. We race and then wait our turn, sandwiched between two other women who have been a couple for many years, and two teenagers having a shotgun wedding.

Ray is the one who performs the weddings in the little makeshift chapel, complete with an arbor with leaves, a ring pillow, and an assistant named Loon, who takes pictures and fills out the marriage license. Loon asks if we have a camera. Just my cell phone, we tell him. He takes it and clicks away as Ray, glowing with joy, reminds us of all of our years together and blesses us for the years to come, coaching us on our vows to love each other in sickness and in health, in richness and in poverty.

We laugh out loud at the last one. With two kids in college, a grandson in preschool, and a mortgage that depends on my salary, which I lost two weeks ago when I was laid off after nearly 25 years with my company, this particular vow has immediate relevance.

Ray and Loon hand us our paperwork, a personal card addressed to us both and signed by both of them wishing us joy on our wedding day, and a certificate of marriage with a flowered border and all the official parts filled in. We share hugs and goodbyes.

Next is the wedding dinner. Heading out of the courthouse, we notice we are starving and stop at Judy's, the Polish dog stand on the corner. We explain the significance of this meal, and Judy prepares the best Polish dogs we've ever eaten plus a hot dog for little Jamal, whom we were picking up from preschool in half an hour.

We race to the parking garage, where we circle five times looking for the exit where we can pay our parking fee and use that proof of payment to exit the garage. Finally we stop a man and his son to ask directions. He tells us to stay put and sends his son upstairs to pay our parking fee. It turns out that they, too, are celebrating: The son has just been released from truancy charges brought on by frequent absences due to his diabetes. The four of us celebrate our good luck today, and they wish us a happy life as we drive away.

En route to get Jamal, we send our wedding pictures to family and friends (all of whom are straight) and immediately get back heartfelt congratulations! This includes a call from my 86-year-old mom in her nursing home. (My dad contracted Parkinson's in 2002; he is full blown into the disease now and barely talks or recognizes anyone).

In between calls, Stacy and I recall the exorbitant financial and emotional cost to our family of life without the fundamental civil right of marriage:

thousands of dollars trying to replicate marriage protections for our family with powers of attorney, legal guardianship of the children for Stacy, and later the co-adoption legal process for her; the years she has to explain and prove herself for doctor, dentist, and teacher appointments; the intrusion of each investigation into our lives of adoption, guardianship, co-adoption; the assault we experience as we turn into our street and see the election signs telling passersby to "Protect Marriage" by voting in two weeks to amend the state constitution and make same-sex marriage illegal again.

We arrive home with our grandson — he's spending the weekend with us — to a bouquet of bright yellow roses from my best friend Nancy.

"Who did that?" Jamal wants to know. We tell him, "Nancy and" — thinking of all the "gifts" of this wedding — "a lot of other people we don't even know." Then we sit on the floor with him to race Lightning McQueen and Doc Hudson cars around the track. Neither of us can imagine a happier honeymoon.

A Black Man Is Elected

BARB

I never get past the shock of the Iowa caucus. Channel surfing, not even intending to watch, Stacy and I sit spellbound as Iowa, of all places (our prejudice, yet again!), votes for Obama.

Stacy holds her breath when Jeremiah Wright, ordained in the same denomination as she is, holds forth. We listen, hearts in our throats, to Obama's 37-minute history of race in America. It's like a poem, no word wasted, every one perfectly saying what it says. We also recognize ourselves in the "older generation" of Jeremiah Wright and others, who have fought many battles and think that nothing will ever change. We switch to MSNBC where we can watch Rachel Maddow, a Rhodes scholar and out lesbian, make hopeful sense of the lead-up and final elections. We get a sneaking suspicion that something huge has shifted, that it's not just a "one-off" but a true sea change: ice turning to water and flowing, water turning to steam and rising ....

We watch the election returns with friends. Twenty people are gathered round, half Black, half "other," half straight, half gay. We are beside ourselves with joy at Obama's election. We stop and pray for his safety.

Whew, Marriage Is Safe Again ... From What?

BARB

Less joyful is our response — the very same night — to the passage of Proposition 8, which changes the California Constitution to eliminate the right of same-sex couples to marry. It states that only a marriage between a man and a woman is valid or recognized in California. Unlike its earlier twin, the Knight Initiative (a.k.a. Proposition 22) in 2000, which passed by 23 percent, Proposition 8 passes by a majority of just 4 percent. Some of our friends are celebrating the progress.

The Mormon church donated 40 percent of the funds to back the proposition, despite the fact that their members make up less than 2 percent of the state's population. That amount came to more than $8 million — eight times more than the next highest donor.

Are we still married? We don't even know. We learn from our tax person that we'll have to file a married return in California and single returns for the IRS, and that it will cost us quite a bit more for her to sort all this out for us. She also says that she and her female partner did not get married for just this reason, though they've been together more than 15 years.

A Never-Ending Field of Sunflowers

STACY

From his birth in November 2004 until this very minute, when he's about to turn 4, Jamal is the most wonderful and uplifting child to be around! No matter what's going on, he makes us laugh. He brings us right into the present and reminds us that this is what really matters: love and connection. The rest will work itself out, one way or another!

Obama Aside, It's Not Over Yet

BARB

Obama's election is a tremendous step forward. Yet to the dismay of many, including academics doing the research on racism, the election is being used to "prove" there's no more discrimination in America, it's ancient history. In fact, all the infrastructure of racism — segregated schools and communities — and the ways of perceiving that lock us into our small lives, remain intact and are able now to flourish because there's "proof" that there's no problem. This denial is what's "proof" — proof that there's a long row to hoe before we get to freedom.

Speaking of Never-Ending ...

BARB

Stephen, now 19, is home today from college. I am overjoyed to see him and in dread of his being here because he constantly gets stopped for what we've started to call DWB — Driving While Black. Sadly, our son is at great risk, right here in his hometown, simply because he is big and Black and male.

When I hear sirens, my stomach lurches — Stephen's home so the police could be after him. Sure enough, he calls within thirty minutes to say he's been pulled over on a local street. He is ordered out of the car by an Asian-American officer, who is soon joined by other police officers in more police cars. Stephen is reaching for his license when the officers start screaming at him to lie down on the wet ground facedown. With guns drawn, they search him and his car.

The police tell Stephen they stopped him because they first thought he was the young man they were looking for (a friend of Stephen's who they say has committed a robbery), and then, when Stephen scratched his neck, the original officer thought he was signaling to people hidden in the backseat of his car. When the officers realize Stephen has told the truth and isn't who they are looking for and isn't hiding the young man in his car, they thank him, shake his hand, and let him go.

I am a wreck, thinking of guns drawn on my boy. What is happening in this town? Of course we call the friend's mom, knowing she'll be very worried that the police are looking for her son. The mom spends all afternoon sorting out this mess. Turns out the cops aren't looking for her son at all, but for another boy with a different name who looks nothing like either her son or ours, though they are all Black.

I think constantly of Amartya Sen, the Nobel economist, and his point that a Black boy born in America lives in an "undeveloped" country. To see our upper-middle-class white college town as an undeveloped part of the world is not far off the mark. To think that I live in a developed country and my son in an undeveloped country, both under the same roof, is at the moment, once again, more than I can bear.

Is it Just Us? Is it Just Our Town?

BARB

A grim comfort through all our trials is that we are not the only family this is happening to.

- A white mom and dad with two pregnant teens decide to go back to Europe, forfeiting his appointment at a prestigious local university, because they feel they can't raise healthy kids in this country.

- Cary and Al (she a poet and Caucasian, he a professional athlete, former police detective, and African-American), along with their kids and their daughter's boyfriend, are held at gunpoint face down in their own front yard while swearing police ransack their home, a vicious police dog barks and lunges, and police helicopters circle overhead. Finally the police haul the boyfriend away in handcuffs while the neighbors in deck chairs look on, giving interviews about the family to the local newspaper. Eventually, the parents and their kids are allowed off the ground. Two days later, the boyfriend is released for lack of evidence. Later, when Cary and Al contact the police auditor with their story of the excessive force used, the police investigate their own behavior and find excessive force was not used.

- A lawyer tells us it's an unwritten law in the next town over that all Blacks are to be stopped and questioned because "We don't want them here in our town." (Never mind that — as in our town — Blacks own homes and live there.)

These aren't one-off cases. This is systemic and pervasive racism, and it's happening below the radar of fair-minded white citizens who haven't had a brush with it through Black friends or family. We *must* find a way to make someone who can change things look into the pattern of harassment against Blacks in our town.

The Last Straw —
Though of Course It's Not

BARB

Stephen is home visiting from college again when he has a minor car accident. He skids into a fire hydrant during the first rain of the season, reports it immediately, meets with a police officer at our home, and promises to pay for the damage to the hydrant. He is given a tiny square Post-It note with a case number on it — no ticket is issued.

Five days later, having heard nothing official yet about a ticket or the cost of the hydrant, Stacy calls the local police to follow up. (Stephen is now back at college in Southern California.) She speaks with an officer who finds the case number and says it will be a while before the city sends us a bill. He says we have done everything necessary.

Two weeks later, we are shocked to receive a letter from the chief of police stating that she has received a warrant for our son's arrest. Apparently, Stephen is being charged with hit and run. How do you commit a hit and run when you have called the police to report your accident? We contact the chief to say there must be some mistake. The chief emails us back, confirming that the officer who took Stephen's report has clearly indicated that our son reported the accident within 30 minutes of its happening. The next day, the chief contacts us again, this time to say the district attorney has agreed to drop the charges and dismiss the warrant if we will send proof that Stephen has auto insurance and will pay for the damage to the hydrant. We provide this information the same day. Whew, we think, another bullet dodged.

Over the course of the next two months, it is discovered that the police chief had instructed officers to routinely stop African-Americans to ask what they are doing in town, check their licenses and send them home if they don't live here. Enough folks are scandalized by this that she resigns.

Shortly afterward, we are dumbfounded to receive a copy of an arrest warrant for Stephen, charging him with hit and run. We email and call, leaving messages for the new acting chief of police, asking what in the world is going on. There is no response. Stacy takes time off work to go to the station with copies of the former police chief's email telling us the warrant has been rescinded.

The acting chief refuses to see us but sends us an email. He says the district attorney has refused to rescind the arrest warrant for Stephen.

I feel ill. Again. All these weeks, while we have been assuming our son was legally in the clear, the warrant for his arrest remained in place. Stephen has been driving around subject to immediate arrest and the ensuing trauma and expense, and none of us even knew it.

I have a long phone conversation with the acting chief, asking question after question after question: Are you looking to arrest our son? What is the meaning of this warrant from your perspective? What does it mean that the bail is $2,000? What is it you hope to achieve by nullifying the earlier decisions made by the chief of police and district attorney?

The acting chief recommends that we pay for the fire hydrant (we still haven't received a bill for it and cannot pay without the bill), and that Stephen present himself at the local police station, where he will be fingerprinted and formally charged. Eventually, he says, Stephen and our lawyer can present his side in court, and hopefully they will be able to plead down to an infraction.

Stacy and I do not see why any of this is necessary, other than paying for the fire hydrant. We decide to deal with this situation in the court of public opinion — if not a court of law — as an example of the much larger and pervasive problem of harassment of Black youth in our town.

We don't believe the D.A. just changed his mind. As the acting chief says, this is not a big case in the scheme of things. It is certainly not anything a D.A. would have to ponder and then change his mind about. We think our local police department did something to reverse the previous chief's decision and to help the D.A. change his mind. We'd like to know who did this, what they did, and why they did it.

We plan a meeting with other mixed-race and Black families who feel similarly frightened and out of faith with our local police department, along with several knowledgeable community activists, to see what we can do to stop what we perceive to be the systemic harassment and intimidation of our African-American sons.

We write up our stories (and another family writes up theirs), and we appear before the Human Relations Commission twice, meet with the city manager once, and talk to the newspapers three times. We get support and questions, and everyone is very nice. However, nothing at all changes, despite promises in writing to the contrary.

The acting chief is a handsome white ex-jock, charming and personable. Over the weeks and months, we come to realize that although he was brought in to replace the previous chief, who resigned as a result of allegations of racism, he is even worse than she was. After all, she acknowledged the racist treatment and undid its consequences for us. Under his watch, on the other hand, all her work is undone and our son is at risk again.

We join others in pointing out the issues with this acting chief before the Human Relations Commission and in the newspaper, but after a nationwide search he's confirmed with great fanfare.

Sadly, about the same time, Stephen comes in to the local police station with me, where he is photographed, fingerprinted and booked for hit and run. This is a heart-breaking and shameful experience for both of us. I am ashamed of my city and my country — and of myself that I could not save him from this. He is ashamed because he is being booked and is going to jail. He and I both know this is happening because he is Black. For hitting a fire hydrant and reporting it, there is no way that I nor any other white citizen would in a million years ever be booked for "hit and run" with warrants following us everywhere and jail looming ahead.

Writing ... the Rock Will Wear Away

BARB

Stacy joins me in writing our story. We pull out journals, files, emails — the paper trail of our lives — and take turns remembering, committing to the page the ups and downs of raising our kids.

The kids themselves are amused by our latest project. To them, it's just one more thing we're doing that isn't going to change anything — don't we understand this? We assure them we do understand how hopeless it feels that anything in our town could change, but we remind them of the song we sang to them when they were little, "Can we be like drops of water falling on the stone ... as time goes by, the rock will wear away."

I remind them that in the town where I grew up, Black and white people couldn't even use the same drinking fountain, or go to the same school, or sit together in the movies, or sit together on the bus. That Stacy and I could never have openly lived together — let alone have gotten married, even for a few months — nor could we ever have had the children we were meant to have: them! That those of us who tried to change things back then were afraid for our lives because guys with guns were out there looking for us. We remind them that things do change, often for the better, even in our lifetimes.

Shawna and Stephen remain unconvinced but indulgent. They give us permission to tell our story as we see it, as long as we change their names and they don't have to read the book!

Globalization Locally ... and Kings

BARB

My company has been outsourcing jobs for over a decade now, and I've managed to dodge the bullet. After 24 years and 10.5 months, just six weeks short of 25 years and much better retirement benefits, I am laid off.

I appeal four times to get the layoff delayed for six weeks — something that is routinely occurring all over the company for personal or business reasons, both of which I cite and document strong cases for. In my case, however, the various managers to whom I appeal are too new, scared or faithful to the computer-generated layoff list to do the decent thing. After exhausting all appeals (in fact, there are none, just time-honored steps to go through that are no more than useless artifacts of an earlier era in corporate America), I am laid off and more than ready to go.

I am astonished at the social capital the company squanders by treating employees like this. Even if quarterly spreadsheet thinking produces these layoffs, as top management claims, doesn't someone on top realize we are potential customers and influence potentially hundreds more?

Subsequent history will prove not one of the folks now on top will stick around long enough to see the consequences of treating people this way. The numbers prove that a huge reason the company cannot afford its employees is that executives are taking home an ever higher percentage of the profits. In the years I've been working, executive pay has increased from 40 to 80 times that of the average worker to more than 1,000 times that wage.

The new feudalism is absolute, and some of the new kings are richer than any before them in history — and, in their own ways, just as cruel.

Moving Back ... and Forward

BARB

Without my job, we can no longer afford our home here. So we move back to the city where we had our first home 30 years ago, the place where we could not find jobs and so had to move away from.

We come to see the forced move as a blessing. People here are much kinder and more diverse. In retrospect, the nice white liberal town where we raised our children seems like a giant iceberg, floating far from the mainland, full of sharp edges, freezing cold and blindingly white. Our new community feels like a festival. Lots of music, warmth, color, eye-contact, laughter and tears, with new friends and foods from all over the world. Another miracle for us.

Life Goes On

BARB

When Shawna graduated from high school, she won an award — created expressly for her — for courage and persistence. These traits persist through the subsequent years. She is proud of herself and is coming to terms with her life. Several times she says, "Mom, just so you know, I don't believe in God. If there was a God, Jamal would still be alive." I admit that my own belief in God, as I once thought of God, is gone. I don't believe in a kind and powerful father in the sky either. "And yet," I tell her, "while we don't believe in God, we can still believe in miracles. Who could have ever predicted that in the depths of despair, having lost your soul mate, you would still finish high school, win an award for courage, become a good mom and be successful in college?" She concedes that maybe she believes in miracles.

Shawna's miracles continue over the next few years. Her dream to become a social worker and open a home for unwed teen moms is on its way to becoming a reality. "I could really help girls in this situation because I've been through it myself," she says. College is the same uphill climb that school has always been, but her courage and persistence continue, and she wins a scholarship to finish. The courses rack up, and she's on track to complete community college with three associate degrees and a B average.

We remain very involved in Shawna's life. Because of her learning disability, she's legally entitled to tutoring in every class, but the state is bankrupt and there are no tutors. We read along with her in every class and talk through with her all the ideas she has for the many papers required. It's a half-time job between Stacy and me. Shawna is so bright, insightful and organized! We are learning and growing together.

Shawna falls in love with a fellow student. We like him very much: He's bright, articulate, a miracle who's survived the worst neighborhood in our state. Soon they are pregnant, once again on purpose. To Shawna's shock, her boyfriend soon takes off, moving across the country. Shawna is enraged and bitter. Now she is in school full-time, with a difficult pregnancy. She is sick all the time and has to get intravenous hydration twice a week at the hospital. But she never misses a class, a test or a paper.

Shawna's second beautiful baby boy is born. On Justin's third day of life, still in the hospital, we learn that he has heart disease and will have to have open-heart surgery in three or four months for tetralogy of Fallot, a complicated condition with a hole in his heart and valves switched around. Shawna, Jamal Jr., and Justin move into our tiny townhouse while we keep a vigil over the baby for the next few months until surgery. We decide to keep Jamal in the same preschool — despite its distance from our home — for the sake of continuity in his life, which is otherwise topsy-turvy with a new baby brother and living with his grandparents.

The enervating dread we are all feeling exhausts us. Shawna is convinced the baby will die in surgery. We tell her we are convinced he will not, and point to the skill of the doctors, the guarded assurances they've given us, and the fact that they successfully do hundreds of these surgeries a year.

My own doubts and fears I let myself feel by sobbing every single weekday during the 45-minute drive home from little Jamal's preschool. Stacy and I both experience our fears as well at night: We are having nightmares and getting very little sleep.

Justin's doctors are fabulous and the surgery goes well. Recovery is actually a joy. Justin grows like a weed now that he has oxygen in his blood and can move, kick, yell and eat everything in sight. His mom is his favorite person on earth, with his big brother a close second. To our joy, we are next in his lineup of favorites.

Stephen heads back to college, where he is majoring in culinary arts. Before long he has taken a number of culinary classes from the best schools on the East and West coasts, and in the Midwest too! He decides to stay in the big city of his last school and start work. There are no jobs to be found. He keeps at it, even as he parties a lot and is racking up speeding tickets that scare us all — himself included.

We continue to support everyone on our shrinking savings, grateful that we have been able to put something aside for retirement, frightened that it's going to be gone before we will need it for ourselves. But the miracles continue.

Stacy's mother gives us money just at the point we most need it. After a lot of paperwork, Barb's insurance covers Justin's surgery. Stephen calls to tell us that the business cards he's scattered all over town are paying off. He has just agreed to cater a dinner for 100 people! We hold our breath, wondering how on earth he'll do it. He calls, triumphant: He served steak, chicken and sausage, two salads and the flan for which he won an award in school. People love his food and say they'll call him again.

American Family ... Call and Response

BARB

Stacy and I publish the first printing of *American Family: Things Racial*, which concludes right after Obama's election. We send it out to friends, who read it and send it along to their friends. The response is overwhelming: positive and energizing, with requests for us to bring the book up to date with the present —Barb's layoff, selling the house and moving, Justin's surgery — and to say a bit more about our own transformation. It shocks us in a good way, that a few of our African-American friends see the book as hopeful, a story of triumph! We have to sit a few months with this one before it begins to make sense to us.

We are overjoyed at the process the book is in. It's begun to feel like the call and response of the Black church, which we so loved at Jamal's funeral and have experienced many times in Black churches since. Our first printing of the book was a call. The comments in the front of the second printing (this one) are excerpts from the overwhelming response. This second printing is a second call and includes changes that represent a great labor of love: Adam Kahane's wonderful foreword, our friend Jay Davidson's meticulous edits (some of which I've undoubtedly failed to incorporate), Margot Silk Forrest's always thoughtful and loving edits, and Ken Homer's heartfelt and deeply provocative questions for self-study and group work.

We get on with this printing of the book, writing the chapters following "The Last Straw" and making some changes to earlier chapters.

Stacy and I rejoin the 12-step fellowships we immersed ourselves in years ago in order to free ourselves from bad habits and become totally present for starting and raising a family. Family raised: mission accomplished — as much as it ever is for any parent. Now we've come full circle: back again in 12-step programs to free ourselves and become present for stepping up to more as the call and response continues through this printing of *American Family*, our website (www.thingsracial.com), workshops, speaking, networking and helping others engaged in fulfilling the promise of the American dream of liberty and justice for all God's children.

Transformation ...

BARB

Several people who read the first printing of *American Family* ask us to say more about how the experience of raising our children has transformed us. We begin our next draft of the book by putting into words our immediate, gut-reaction response to the question of how we've been transformed:

Raising our kids has transformed us from who we were before kids: upbeat, physically healthy, optimistic white liberals with just enough incidents of involvement in civil rights to give us the creds to do nothing more, to who we are now after raising our kids: disillusioned, frequently angry, often demanding, at times quite unpleasant, righteous and sometimes despairing, chain-smoking, over-eating, and occasionally heavy drinkers. And we are now back in 12-step programs to recover from the bad habits into which we've drifted with each Mack Truck and disillusionment. Transformation! Let's hear it for transformation!

This makes us laugh, and then gives us pause on account of its cynicism. Our second response is to sit longer with the question, not knowing the answer. We notice, to our surprise — and, in fact, to our cautious wonder — that we are in a different place after having gotten others' responses to our book.

We had had a hard time finishing the first printing of the book because in order to finish we had to reread it, and we were already exhausted from living the story. We couldn't bear to read it again, let alone again and again. So the book took years to complete, and then when we finally finished writing it, we did nothing with it for another three years because we thought the story was too depressing. We figured no one would be able to stand reading it any more than we could, and if they did, they would be no better for it.

But then, out of nowhere it seemed to us, Eric Holder, our attorney general, put into words what we had been thinking for years:

> "Though this nation has proudly thought of itself as an ethnic melting pot, in things racial we have always been and continue to be ... a nation of cowards ... Though there remain many unresolved racial issues in this nation, we, average Americans, simply do not talk enough with each other about race."

We watched what happened when he said these words: He was pilloried by just about everyone. *Were we up for that?* we asked ourselves. On the other hand, we thought, we didn't have nor were we seeking his audience, all of America. What if our book were aimed at just liberal Americans, to help us talk to each other about race and move forward with the insights born of these conversations? What if our book would do more good in the hands of people who wanted it than sitting in manuscript form on a shelf in our house? And what if we got it out right away and let others help us figure out how to make it useful?

So we self-published *American Family* and sent it out to friends, who in turn sent it to their circle of contacts. And what we hoped would happen, happened. Those who read it help us take the story further. Our readers affirmed our story as a contribution. As one put it, "Truth is the only place to start, and you've given us a truth about racism in a liberal town, a truth many good people — and here I include myself — do not know and will benefit from knowing."

Another thing that happened was that several of our readers even thought the book was a story of hope! At first this really puzzled us. But when we sat long enough with it, we began to understand, perhaps in part because of the spiritual work we were doing in our 12-step programs. We began to notice hope, in the form of new friends and new ideas, coming into our living room and taking a seat right next to despair over the racism that surrounds us all.

Of course, our old friend Despair still refuses to budge. It sits there, solid and entrenched in its big old easy chair, determined to stay for the duration.

But Hope has somehow crept in on little cat feet. It hops up on the arm of Despair's fat chair and nestles in for a short visit ... or maybe a longer stay?

... One Day at a Time

STACY

> Very much like alcoholism [and] drug addiction, racism ... is a disease and we are in perennial recovery and relapse. So you have to get up every morning and struggle against it.
>
> — Cornel West, *Breaking Bread: Insurgent Black Intellectual Life*

> We are at a crucial crossroad in the history of this nation — and we either hang together by combating these forces that divide and degrade us or we hang separately. Do we have the intelligence, humor, imagination, courage, tolerance, love, respect, and will to meet the challenge? Time will tell. None of us alone can save the nation or world. But each of us can make a positive difference if we commit ourselves to do so.
>
> — Cornel West, *Race Matters*

Our third response to the question of how raising our kids has transformed us arises over the next few months. We begin a long period of rumination on Cornel West's observation that racism is like an addiction.[13] Since we're in 12-step meetings for our bad habits (and the programs are working; the habits are dropping away), it's no great leap to imagine a new program, Racists Anonymous — a spiritual program to end racism in America and eventually the world, one person at a time. Is this a crazy idea? We muse on ....

Okay, let's start with Cornel West's insight: Racism is an addiction. Like all other addictions, it's fraught with ignorance, denial and pain. Sometimes it leads to death. And like other addictions, it's possible to recover from racism, or at least to be in recovery, one day at a time, in a circle with others. *How might Racists Anonymous work?* we wonder. Based on our own "experience, strength and hope," which is the only basis from which to speak in 12-step programs, here's how we think Racists Anonymous might work (and how this proposed process is already working for us).

First of all, as in all 12-step programs, the most important word in each of the steps ("we") is assumed before the specific wording of the step. For example, step one in Alcoholics Anonymous is "Admitted we were powerless over alcohol, that our lives had become unmanageable." In the steps we offer below, we'll include that all-important word as a reminder. Recovery from racism absolutely requires "we" — *no one* can do this alone. It has to be done through local circles of support, as in all 12-step meetings. But the circles could start in book clubs, church groups, or ad hoc gatherings. They could use

---

[13] *Breaking Bread: Insurgent Black Intellectual Life* by bell hooks and Cornel West (South End Press, 1999)

the conversation guidelines we offer in "An Invitation to Conversation" at the end of this book as a way of discovering racism in each member's own history and in current situations where formerly they thought there was none. Then, once racism is accepted as real in one's experience, the 12-step process could begin.

Here are the steps for Racists Anonymous, as we envision them: a path to national and eventually global transformation, one step and one person at a time.

1. **We admitted we were powerless over racism, that our lives had become unmanageable.**

    Taking ourselves as an example, writing our book turns out to have been our step 1. From one perspective, our whole book is one example after another of our powerlessness over racism and how unmanageable our lives have become as a result of denying both our powerlessness *and* our own racism — out of ignorance at times, out of stubbornness at others. We are completely demoralized as we sit down to take our first step, writing the book, and we write it only as a way to stop crying or sinking deeper into despair. Admitting that our good jobs, white privilege, activist backgrounds, ability to work the system — that all of this still leaves us powerless to protect our children from the devastation of racism is a great cry of anguish and also a huge relief.

    Hope arrives when we face the truth. It will take something much more than all the privilege and force of will that parents can bring to the table to protect their children from racism, because racism is systemic. It is rooted in our collective denial, unconsciousness, ill- and sometimes good will, all instantiated in time-honored practices, policies and processes at local, state and national levels, and it is bred into personalities and character. The power of racism, as has been said in 12-step circles for other addictions, is truly "cunning, baffling and powerful."

Our personal experience of racism can connect to the national level when we simply reflect in our circle on the day's news. For example, as we write, the hot topic is the president's birth certificate and Harvard credentials. We bring this up in one of our own support circles.

To her own horror, one of us in the circle (white) has actually found herself wondering if Obama was really born here. She immediately realizes she would never be thinking such a thing about a white president. Several members recall that when the news comes on with another round of questions about Obama's credentials, they just switch channels. As a circle, we talk about what underlies each of these responses: wondering, horror, switching channels. We consider what "right action" would truly be in this situation. What else is possible, and what does each person in the circle think about it?

We consider how this question of the president's credentials is undermining the country by deflecting our attention from other matters, like the three wars we're in, the lack of healthcare, the ongoing destruction of our public school system and the directly proportional growth of the prison system, the destruction of the environment, the erosion of our infrastructure, and persistent high unemployment. We move on to discuss what each of us is doing on these other issues ... and wonder if this, in fact, is the best response to the credentials drama: simply to ignore it and work on other things. Or does ignoring it mean colluding with the distraction it causes? What will be best for our children and grandchildren? we ask each other.

Why is admitting our powerlessness so important? Because we cannot have meaningful conversations and take authentic, justice-making action without a clear-eyed look at what is true: As individuals and as a country, we are in the grip of racism. Facing this fact is, we feel, the primary purpose of our own first step, writing and publishing *American Family*. The questions listed in "An Invitation to Conversation" at the end of this book can enable people to understand racism and denial enough to claim it in their history and look at their own current powerlessness. At this point they're ready for the first step of Racists Anonymous, if they choose to go further into recovery from racism for themselves and the country. Admitting powerlessness enables each of us not to flinch, not to spare, not to sugar-coat the situation, and to do so long enough to consider *what is really going on.*

When we admit we are powerless, we overcome our personal denial that there is a problem, and in time we overcome the larger, systemic denial — even, and in the case of our own town, especially, among white liberals. Incident by incident, well-meaning people can argue that it's not so bad. But taken together, all these incidents constitute evidence from our own lives that racism is killing us individually and as a country.

Like many who have argued with us over the years, we started out positive, seeing each incident as an anomaly, a "one-off." But what actually happened to us was evolution in the other direction. We started out thinking that we could take on systemic racism, that our savvy, energy and experience would enable us to spare our children the ravages of racism. We were terribly wrong. We now experience the paradox of being in despair while still having a dawning hope that authentic change is possible. Our story is far from over, and in good call-and-response fashion, we hope you will help us create a different story for all of us.

Our complete bafflement at the response of those of our Black friends who saw *American Family* as a message of hope now begins to make sense to us in light of the 12 steps. *Admitting our despair and defeat at tackling racism in our town is the first step to moving beyond despair and defeat.* Truly, we now know much more about the size and scale of systemic racism at a local level in a liberal town. We see clearly now that only the process of changing one person at a time, in circles of conversation and support, can enable us to change one town at a time, which eventually will grow into an America with justice and liberty for all.

2. **We came to believe that a power greater than ourselves could restore us to sanity.**

For Barb and me, a transcendent, benign and all-powerful God is no longer the Higher Power of our own personal understanding. The power greater than ourselves, in our experience right now, is our circles, loosely defined as (to use the language of our childhood religions) "where two or more are gathered together in My Name." For us, this means the large circle of those who have responded to our book, who are engaged in reflection on racism and who are engaged in action to end it.

These circles constitute a power greater than ourselves, a power that is slowly but surely restoring us to sanity. We begin to understand the paradox that we could feel so hopeless about our story while some readers see it as hopeful. As Barb has said often about our lives, "The truth can hurt, but the lies will make you crazy. I'd rather be hurt than crazy."

3. **We made a decision to turn our will and our lives over to the care of our Higher Power[14] as we understand our Higher Power.**

For us, we trust our growing circle to help us discern our own path forward. On the one hand, we must make a living. We are well credentialed to go back into corporations and make the money we need to keep our kids in college, our grandkids in school and ourselves okay in our eventual retirement. On the other hand, we want to be open to whatever we can do, as it evolves from working our first and second steps, to continue the journey with *American Family*, the book, the circles, workshops, the talks, whatever and however we can. So far, we have not discovered or discerned a business model that yields a living out of our *American Family* work — as one of our friends often reminds us, "Hope is not a strategy!"

---

[14] We are using "Higher Power" throughout these steps instead of "God."

So far we are doing this work without charge. In fact, we are funding it ourselves because we so much want it to be done. We have covered all the costs of doing a book, including editing, artwork and printing; and with our dear friend and colleague Diane Woods, we have subsidized almost entirely the costs of doing workshops, including consulting, customizing, delivery, evaluation and follow up. Clearly this business model is not sustainable. How we will support ourselves doing this work remains a mystery. But we are finding that just putting it out there has begun to illuminate options that we could never have imagined on our own. We will keep you posted through our website, www.thingsracial.com, as solutions unfold. We welcome any suggestions you may have.

4. **We made a searching and fearless inventory of ourselves.**

We continue to learn daily about our gifts and our shortcomings through our anti-racism work. It's humbling to be in our 60s and still be discovering the subtle ways we ourselves perpetuate racism even as we're trying to overcome it. For example, we've had to acknowledge our lack of humility in assuming we could protect our children from racism. That assumption sometimes got in the way of our recognizing that while we had shocking abundance and power because of the gift of white privilege, these weren't enough for us to counter the equally shocking depth and breadth of systemic racism without help. We now profoundly know this is work we must do with others. This discovery has allowed us to respect and honor — in ourselves and others — the enormous courage and persistence it takes, one day at a time, day after day, year after year to do the work implied in a Racists Anonymous program or something like it.

5. **We admitted to our Higher Power, to ourselves and to another human being the exact nature of our wrongs.**
This is what we are doing in our various support circles.

6. **We were entirely ready to have our Higher Power remove all these defects of character.**
We are finding that our shortcomings disappear through the work of our circles — making room for a whole new batch to be revealed! For example, through the circle of those appreciating our first step (writing and publishing the book), the shortcoming of despair is now tempered with hope, allowing for action in the form of getting the next printing of the book out. This, in turn, is revealing the shortcoming of our introversion (yet again), now in the form of the hesitation and procrastination we experience about accepting the speaking and preaching invitations we have received. We overcome these hesitations and accept: We're traveling out of state next month to speak — whereupon, no doubt, new shortcomings will be revealed!

7. **We humbly asked our Higher Power to remove our shortcomings.**
In our circles committed to anti-racism work, we ask that the circle hold the intention that our shortcomings be removed. And it works. For example, Barb asks Pathwalkers, a group she's been doing for 10 years, to hold the intention for a month that her

shortcoming of not asking for what she really wants be removed. She is then able to admit to herself that what she *really* wants for the next printing of this book is for Adam Kahane to write the foreword. This is an outlandish wish, she admits. She's met him only once, over twenty years ago, when they both ducked out of a conference at the same time, then talked for four hours about anti-racism work. She's followed his work ever since, and has emailed him exactly twice over the years, most recently to express appreciation for his latest book.

Having put the shortcoming "not asking for what I really want" out to the group, and asking them to hold the intention that this shortcoming be removed, Barb makes her "outlandish" request to Adam. It turns out he is traveling in Africa, so there is no time to mail the book to him and expect him to read it and respond. Barb defaults to another shortcoming, giving up too soon on things she wants: She assumes Adam's travels signify a "no," and sends him an email saying, "Thank you anyway." Luckily, he does not share this shortcoming. He responds to her thank you by proposing we email the manuscript instead of mailing it. We do, and within a month we have his foreword in our hands.

As for me, I have the same shortcoming of not asking for what I really want. And what I really want are study questions for self-study and self-initiated circle work, beyond the work that Diane and I facilitate (see www.thingsracial.com). I ask my circle to hold this intention. I also talk with Diane about it, and she turns out to have a dear friend of many years who specializes in "collaborative conversations." She says he writes the best questions she's ever pondered. Diane asks her friend, Ken Homer, if he'll read *American Family* and write study questions for us. He does so and is deeply moved by what it brings up for him. Then he creates the magnificent questions in "An Invitation to Conversation."

Such is the power of a circle, and the transformation that can occur when we acknowledge our shortcomings and ask our Higher Power to remove them.

8. **We made a list of all persons we had harmed, and became willing to make amends to them all.**

For us, this step and the following one are ongoing. It's very important, though, to include ourselves in the list of all persons we have harmed through racism. One of the things we have to face is that in our ignorance of racism's vast and persistent nature, and our arrogance in thinking we could protect our children, we have harmed ourselves by constantly throwing ourselves at this brick wall, time and again, to the point of suicidal exhaustion and despair. We have hurt our children by prolonging their bad experiences in our efforts to fix them. We see now there is a better way to fight with racism, and it is as Eric Holder proposes, to begin "as average Americans ... [to] talk with each other... about race." How? Through the circles to which we already belong, and perhaps, in our wildest dreams, through Racists Anonymous circles or something similar that spring up everywhere, in every community and town.

We also try to stay vigilant about examining our assumptions and judgments about others, and, mostly, we make amends as needed. There is also something called "living amends" in addition to verbal amends, which means we set our intention to continue to observe our judgments and change our behavior.

9. **We made direct amends to such people wherever possible, except when to do so would injure them or others.**

   For example, we make amends to ourselves by giving ourselves one afternoon a week when we are unplugged from computers and phones, and unavailable for any emergency or work of any kind. It's fantastic the energy that comes in from this break — energy that is then available for the work. We continue to make amends to our children by showing up for them and, through therapy and reading and circles, continuing to learn more about how best to do that.

10. **We continued to take personal inventory and when we were wrong promptly admitted it.**

    One of our shortcomings is signing up for more than we can deliver without causing great hardship to ourselves and others. For example, today, after working on this book, Barb will call a committee working on fundraising for the all-Black elementary school where she volunteers and admit that she's overcommitted. She'll ask that someone else take over running the committee while we travel out of state next month.

11. **We sought through prayer and meditation to improve our conscious contact with our Higher Power as we understood that Higher Power,**

praying only for knowledge of "right action"[15] for us and the power to carry that out.

We are finding that when we sit in circle at least once a week, somewhere, with the intention of discerning next steps in our anti-racism work, the next steps are revealed to us. On the other hand, when we don't sit in circle or we sit but without this intention, we are soon overwhelmed with an enormous number of "worthwhile secondary activities," as Barb's father used to call the kinds of things she overwhelmed herself with as a child and teenager.

12. **Having had a spiritual awakening as the result of these steps, we tried to carry this message to others who may need what a program like Racists Anonymous could offer, and to practice these principles in all our affairs.**

This spiritual awakening is only possible when the previous 11 steps have been taken. Neither as an individual engaged in this work, nor collectively as a country, can we jump to spiritual awakening as the first order of business in ending racism. We have a lot of legwork to do before that. In addition, spiritual awakening is not a one-time thing. It comes with the struggle and it is ongoing. In healing the addiction of racism, it is as Cornel West says, "You have to get up every morning and struggle against it."

Will Racists Anonymous ever come to pass? We have shared our vision with a few friends including some who've not read the book, and they are excited! As one said just

---

[15] We prefer this term to "His will," which is used in the original 12 steps.

yesterday, "For the first time in my life, I can envision the end of racism in my lifetime!"

Barb then remembers the first sermon I did based on the book (downloadable from www.thingsracial.com). The layperson who introduced me and the topic of racism began her introduction by saying, "My name is Kathy, and I am a racist." Barb recalls that you could hear a pin drop in that church. Kathy went on to share the insights that gave rise to this statement (mapping completely to Ken Homer's questions in the last section of this book). Many in the congregation recognized Kathy's words as the traditional way of introducing oneself in 12-step meetings. After the sermon conversation went on for three hours as people shared their experience, strength and hope. None of us at that time, however, pushed through to the idea of a 12-step program as a means for ongoing recovery from racism.

Could Racists Anonymous become a reality? Barb gets online to see if it already exists somewhere. Based on her very preliminary research, it seems that every few years someone comes up with the idea and writes about their own very moving transformation in light of each of the 12 steps, recast for overcoming the addiction to racism. It does not seem that a recognized program has resulted. Ironically, the closest thing to an ongoing activity under the name "Racists Anonymous" is an effort by several groups who use the term to ridicule liberals in general or anti-racists and African-Americans in particular.

More shall be revealed. One thing we know is that if there is a 12-step program for overcoming racism out there, we will find it. And if there isn't, we will help make it happen if it's time. Whether a 12-step program to end racism ever comes to pass or not, we are quite sure nothing short of a spiritual awakening in this country can free us from the ravages of racism. Perhaps this awakening will transpire in other kinds of circles over time, much as it has done for years in our own lives.

And/or perhaps, as one dear friend mused in her response to the first printing, it will occur as more racist generations die out and are replaced by younger, freer (and, not incidentally, ever more gradually racially mixed) individuals and families and towns.

We believe racism will end. Sometimes, we even experience ourselves in golden moments beyond racism and no racism: slathered with sunscreen on our white skin so we can teach a Black grandbaby (also slathered) to swim in our community pool on a hot day surrounded by all the skin colors of the world; shopping at a flea market; eating a chili-mango as we listen to rap music by white kids and admire the five-month-old mahogany-hued baby girl on her father's shoulder, dancing with him to the music.

So, finally, in response to the question, How has raising your kids transformed you? We're finding that there's no final response. Our transformation is ongoing. It's occurring as we are co-writing with you, through our lives, the story of *American Family*. It isn't something we "get" and then tell you about. It's something we create together.

There's a line out of a movie that says something like, "I'm going to tell you a story and you will tell me how it's going to end." Really, though, there's no end to transformation. We look forward to meeting you in our travels and hearing your stories, your discoveries and the actions you have taken. We imagine great surprises, great learning, and wondrous progress as together we forge an America for all of God's children.

PART V:
HOW TO SUPPORT EACH OTHER AND FAMILIES UNDER SIEGE

Based on our experiences, people generally want to help when someone or a family is in trouble. Often they don't know how. Here are some thoughts, based on our experience of being on the receiving end.

Bottom line and fundamental to all that follows: Sometimes, even though you do your best, we feel diminished by your efforts. When you sense that, you feel diminished too. This seems like a lose-lose situation, best avoided altogether by not reaching out in the first place. Oddly enough, however, even though we may feel diminished, we feel better than if you had avoided us altogether. Diminished is so much better than invisible or contagious!

Here are some more thoughts about what we've found helpful — and not.

1. **Reach out.** Separate the *cause* of ending racism or homophobia or whatever, from the *immediate human outreach* needed by a fellow human being who is *suffering,* and reach out. Our dear friend Yolanda made this point just the other day. Like everyone else in this business of creating a world beyond racism, we are still learning every day!

   In our experience and Yolanda's, if you don't separate the cause from the immediate outreach required in the moment, you won't be able to reach out. And if you can't reach out, you will never build the base and grow the relationships that are needed for the cause.

Here's an example Yolanda shared with us that illustrates this dynamic.

Yolanda has been in a church circle that's been meeting monthly for more than 10 years. One in the group is cracking jokes about her own spiritual progress and lack thereof, keeping everyone in stitches, when out of her mouth pops a racist joke. Yolanda, the only African-American in the group, is stunned but manages to say loudly, "That's not funny." The others are startled, and most keep laughing, though now more softly and uneasily. She repeats, "That's not funny." The group leader quickly changes the topic of conversation and the group moves on. Yolanda is numb and says nothing more.

The person cracking the joke calls Yolanda that evening, ashamed, apologetic, remorseful and chagrined at what has popped out of her mouth. Sobbing, she wonders if she'll ever get over her racist roots. Yolanda tells us after their ensuing conversation, "I love her more than I ever have, and it gave me the energy to take on the rest of the circle."

At the next meeting, Yolanda asks the circle, "What were you thinking when I said, 'That's not funny'? Why did you just keep laughing and talking as if nothing had happened? The racist joke really hurt, but your ignoring me hurt so much more. What was going on with you?"

Yolanda tells us that each person, in one way or another, said they knew it was wrong, but they didn't know what to do. They were "paralyzed," "dumbfounded," "totally embarrassed," and "at a complete loss."

The leader of the groups says that she realizes she could have at least stopped the group to acknowledge, "There are two people really hurting in our group. We need to stop for a moment." Others chime in that this would have helped. At least they could have acknowledged they had no idea what to do next.

Yolanda agrees with the rest of the group that action by the leader would have helped. But why, she persists with the group, did they not do anything? Why did they have no idea what to do?

"Well," says one, "What on earth did you want us to do?"

Yolanda responds quietly, "I just wanted someone to reach out and ask me if I was okay."

"Oh my God," says another person in the group. "You mean just do the simple human thing when another person is in trouble?"

"Yes," says Yolanda. "I may be Black, but before anything I'm human. And I was hurting. And you all are my friends. I'm not expecting you to undo centuries of racism behind the jokes and laughter. I'm just asking that you notice that I'm hurting and reach out."

The group spends the rest of the afternoon exploring the implications of this profound insight: If you don't separate racism from the human beings who are hurting because of it (in this case, both the perpetrator and the victim), then you can't address their pain on a human and personal level. And if you can't do that, you will never have the possibility of forging the kinds of relationships required to take on the more systemic forms of racism in your community.

Once you remember and acknowledge the "other" is a person and is hurting — never mind for just a moment that they are Black or gay or both — you will come out of paralysis and find a human, individual-scale action to take. And as our relationships build and deepen over things at this level, our capacity grows for taking on bigger things at other levels.

Everything else we have to say on this topic of support grows from and depends upon this first simple insight: Above all, reach out to the human who is hurting.

2. **Show up.** No matter how clueless you feel — or are — about what you can do to help, come over and be with us. Don't avoid us. Being discriminated against is rarely contagious! We tend to feel isolated and alone, so your being there really helps. Draw out the conversation so you're literally with us for longer. Say things like, "Could you say more about that? How did that make you feel? Is there anything we can do to help? Is there anything that's helped you before that would help now, if only it would happen?" Once you show up, which is the most important thing, you can work on refining your ways of helping. (Read on.)

3. **Ask lots of questions.** Assume you don't really know what is going on. (You probably don't.) Wonder out loud if you know anything about what we're going through. Share your own experiences of strength and weakness, hope and despair. This is another level of being "with" us. When you look for similarities in your

own life, you draw us back into the human family from which we feel we have been expelled. This may be a matter of you identifying with us as parents, or with the administrators and teachers we deal with, or with the child we're trying to help.

4. **Bring food.** Literally. There's something about being fed during a bad time that works miracles. Every religion recognizes the power of breaking bread together. "One who breaks bread with another" is the original meaning (from Latin) of the word *companion*. Companions are what we need.

5. **Forgive yourself.** You may feel very uncomfortable or awkward, or you may realize you've failed to improve the situation. Forgive yourself! Being with people going through a mess that's outside your experience is not easy. But it's how we all learn and how we can help each other.

6. **Forgive us.** We may and probably will fail to appreciate you in the moment. Worse, we may — in our frustration or fear for our children — lash out at you. Please understand that we're really hurting at the moment, and don't hold it against us. We will get over your mistakes, too.

It is also true that being human in difficult situations like these may vary depending on your demographics (although many of the pointers below will work for anyone trying to help.)

If you are a parent yourself, it helps when you:

- Express sadness or dismay about our situation and ask how you can help: "I'm so sorry. Is there anything I can do to help?" While this is often too open-ended a question to elicit a specific and practical response from us, it does get the conversation going and we really appreciate it.

- Notice disparate treatment. "My (white) kid did the same thing, but they only suspended him/her. Why did they expel your kid?" Notice what is happening around you. When you read or hear of some consequence handed out to a Black child or his/her family, ask yourself, "Would the same thing have happened to a white child in the same situation?"

- Offer to show up with us as we pursue fairness and justice for our child. In the example above, say, "Would you like me to go to the principal with you to ask about this disparity?"

- Look for the good. See if you can find a bright side to the bad situation and suggest it: "Well, s/he may have been kicked out, but s/he wasn't physically hurt (like another kid I know) and s/he didn't hurt another child." Give examples if you can.

If you are a parent yourself, it *doesn't* help when you:

- Express the opinion that you or your child is better than us or ours. This often takes the form of the parent saying, "Well, what's happening to your child isn't happening to ours because we raise our kid in such-and-such a way" or "because our kid knows not to _____." Parents often say this kind of thing because they need to convince themselves that what happened to us could never happen to them. This is human and understandable. That's fine if it's done in private, but when the sentiment is expressed to the parents of the child who is suffering, it's inappropriate and offers no comfort. Besides, it assumes that something we did (or didn't do) caused the problem (not always the case), and that what you do is not only better but has never occurred to us. Talk about rubbing salt in the wound!

- Tell us you know exactly how we feel or equate dissimilar experiences. One time, Stephen was suspended for something much less than the white kids were doing; the white kids were not suspended — a fact not disputed by the staff member who saw the incident. A parent who was trying to be helpful said to us: "We know just how you feel. Our son didn't make first chair in the junior orchestra and we were devastated."

Hey, not making first chair in the orchestra is not the same as being kicked out of school! While we have in common that our hopes for our child are being dashed, one child is going to (unfairly) miss out on a week's worth of basic learning, the other on advanced opportunities, fame and glory. One situation is the source of shame and a smear on a child's school record. The other is a source of disappointment. Please understand the difference.

- Tell us that you can't imagine how hard our life is and you feel so bad for us all. This may sound like sympathy, but it sends us to an even lower rung of hell because it makes us feel isolated and damned. Instead, think of the worst thing you've ever experienced, the time when you felt most isolated and helplessness, and say, "I don't know how it feels to have had your exact experience, but I wonder if it's at all like we felt when ...." When you do this, you're not assuming you know how we feel, and you're not asserting that we are outside the realm of your own human experience. You're asking questions and making connections. Questions and connections are good.

- Tell us that you have to hear both sides before you can decide which side you're on. Like we need a judge and executioner added to the mix? If you need to hear the other side, go hear it, but don't tell us about it. Make your decision and come back if you're with us.

If you're not a parent yourself, it helps when you:

- Give us a break. Literally. Ask, "When can I bring over a home-cooked meal? When can we take you to a movie? When can you spare a night to come to our house for some peace and quiet, an escape? When can we take the kids for an afternoon so you two go get a massage?"

If you're not a parent yourself, it *doesn't* help when you:

- Blame the victim for the incident. Don't tell us, "You create your own reality. What is your part in this?" This is not helpful in situations like ours. Collectively, we all create the reality any one of us is experiencing. Don't dump that responsibility onto one family! Interestingly enough, we have never gotten this response from a European or an African friend. Could the belief that "you create your own reality" be uniquely American? While this can be a useful lens for getting in touch with any overlooked power you may have in a given situation, it is not useful for assigning responsibility for causes like racism and homophobia. While "you create your own reality" can theoretically come from other parents, we have only ever gotten it from people, including friends, who are not parents.

- Blame the victim for not recovering from the incident. This is a variation on the preceding item. Again, while it's theoretically possible another parent could blame the victim, we've only ever gotten it from people, including friends, who are not parents. Please don't ask us, "Are you meditating with soothing music at least once a day?" This question assumes a very different reality than the mixture of triage and crisis control that characterizes the lives of most families we know who are raising Black kids in towns like ours. And please don't ask why our kid is so angry. If your life was one of constant harassment and ongoing disparity with your white friends, wouldn't you be angry, too?

If you're Black, it *doesn't* help when you:

- Tell us it's payback time. This takes the form of comments like, "You're white and you owe me (or you deserve it), you fool." We cannot work out systemic and centuries-old racial inequities and outrages on an interpersonal level. Of course we must not perpetuate the inequities on this level, but we cannot redress them at this level. That's not where or when they occurred. One Black friend (a non-parent) actually laughed at our anguish: "Now you see what it feels like ... which is why I didn't have kids." Implied is, "You naïve fools!" and, "Now it's your turn to feel what it's like." A shorthand version of this one is, "Welcome to my world," like we haven't been living in it since the day we adopted our first child.

If you're white, it *doesn't* help when you:

- Ask us, "Why don't Blacks fix it?" This is a variant of, "Why can't Blacks get it together like the Asians/the Mexicans/the Indians?" This implies that there is something wrong with Blacks or that they deserve what is happening to them. Racism is a large and complex question. There is a lot of research on it, and fine minds have given some great answers. If you're really interested, Google it, buy some books, and read up. Do not go to the big question when a family is wrestling with a specific instance of devastating discrimination. Furthermore, this remark overlooks the fact that unlike other ethnicities in America, Black and white are so intertwined that only together will we ever fix racial discrimination against Blacks. As we said at the beginning of this book, it's not us and them. It's all us.

PART VI:
AN INVITATION TO CONVERSATION

At the beginning of this book is a quote from Attorney General Eric Holder that says, in part, "Average Americans, simply do not talk enough with each other about race." After you have read *American Family: Things Racial,* you may want to open up conversations about race with the important people in your life, but you may be hesitant, unsure of how to proceed or whom to talk with. We asked our friend Ken Homer of Collaborative Conversations (www.collaborativeconversations.com) to advise us on framing conversations about "things racial" with the people who matter in your life. Here are his suggestions.

Creating a Context for a Conversation About Race

One thing that *American Family: Things Racial* makes abundantly clear is that none of us is free of the corrosive effects of racism. Talking about racism may be challenging, but it need not be onerous or terrifying. As Barb and Stacy have pointed out, the first step is admitting that each of us is a racist in our own way. Far from a statement of self-blame, "I am a racist" is a powerful learning stance, because from it we can ask ourselves, *What am I assuming here that may not be serving me, us or the situation?*

It's always helpful when inquiring into complex issues like race and racism to get clear on three things: purpose, intention and desired outcomes. Clarity on these at the outset allows us to check in now and again to make sure we are on track.

- Our purpose is to stimulate you to reflect on how racism impacts your life and to invite you to enter into productive conversations about race with the people in your communities and networks.

- Our intention is that these conversations will ripple out among our networks and create shifts in individual and collective behavior — not necessarily through attempts at coordinating action, rather, through the increased awareness these conversations will surface.

- Our desired outcomes fall into the categories of personal, interpersonal and collective:
  -- Personal: to generate more awareness of how racism shows up in my life and how I respond to it.
  -- Interpersonal: to develop better strategies for coping with racism in my relationships.
  -- Collective: eyes on the prize, to be in service to healing racism and creating more options for harmony among all people.

Ten Things to Bear in Mind When Engaging in Conversations About Racism

1. Racism wounds people in three direct (and numerous indirect) ways:
   - We are all directly affected when we are the targets of racism.

- We are all directly affected when we target others due to racism.
- We are all directly affected when we witness racism.

2. In short, we all suffer from the effects of racism and each of us is, to greater or lesser degree, racist.

3. Among the most powerful antidotes to racism is accepting the unconscious racism within ourselves.

4. Racism's power is fueled by mistrust and fear.

5. Racism's power withers in the face of love, compassion and forgiveness.

6. The best way to bring love, compassion and forgiveness forward is to listen to the stories of racism we each carry without needing to fix those stories or the people sharing them. There is great healing in deep listening.

7. Curiosity is more potent than advice. In talking about racism, nearly everyone will experience an almost overwhelming urge to give advice. Please resist. Substituting curiosity for advice will bring forth far more possibilities for healing. If you find yourself giving advice, instead try saying something like: "Tell me more about that," or "Help me understand why that's important."

8. Dwell in not knowing. Racism is not a problem to be solved. It's far too messy, chaotic and complex to be understood from inside a problem-solution mindset. Most of us, especially men, have been trained to look at the world almost exclusively through the lens of problem-solving. Challenging as it may be, when engaging in conversations about racism, we'll learn

things of immense value if we allow ourselves to keep coming back to a place of not knowing.

9. Begin with the people you can trust. We all need to build our capacity to engage in effective conversations about racism. It's much easier to start with people close to us, where trust already exists.

10. Keep it real and keep it grounded. Speak from your personal experience, not from what you have read or heard from someone else.

Three Ways to Get a Conversation Started

Below are three different approaches for opening up a conversation about racism with people in your life. Each set of four questions/requests serves as a guiding framework for conversation. We have intentionally omitted questions that steer people toward the knee-jerk reaction to "do something," the action-oriented response favored in U.S. culture. Uncomfortable as it may be, it's beneficial to sit with the experience of not knowing. The space of not knowing is vast and includes everything we have never tried before with regard to ending racism. We will never discover these things if we can't sit for some time in a place of "not knowing."

Begin with whichever of these three approaches appeals to you the most. If you are able, try each to see how it feels and notice what changes as you work with the different approaches.

We recommend that you not attempt more than one approach in a day. These are simple questions, but the work of answering them is unsparing. Move, stretch, walk around, journal and take breaks. Take care of yourself and take care of each other as you engage here. Allow space and time to integrate your learning. Stay in touch with each other for support. A conversation today may bring up something you'll need a friend to talk through tomorrow.

We invite you to gather some friends together, meet in a safe, comfortable space, share food, look into each other's eyes and listen with your heart to what each one says as you answer the questions. Then, if you feel like it, please share your experiences at www.thingsracial.com.

A First Possible Approach

1. How has racism wounded you?
2. How has racism made you stronger?
3. What is a forgiveness you are withholding due to racism?
4. How are you generating and sharing compassion?

A Second Possible Approach

1. How has racism wounded you?
2. How have you healed those wounds?
3. What is the healing you bring to others suffering from racist wounds?
4. What forgiveness lies between you and your desired relationship with racism?

A Third Possible Approach

1. Tell a story from a time when you first felt the impact of racism in your life.
2. Tell a story from a much more recent time when you felt the impact of racism in your life.

3. What has changed for you in the interval between these times?

4. What arises for you in reflecting on this?

ACKNOWLEDGMENTS

Above all, we want to thank our daughter and son, who have opened up new worlds for us, taught us so much and given us permission to tell this story.

There is no way to acknowledge all of the people who have kept the two of us on the planet for the last 25 years. Many of you will find yourselves in these stories. Things are getting better, and because of you, we are alive to see it. We thank the various circles that have kept us going: Pathwalkers for Barb, the Bay Zen Center for Stacy, and IDK for both of us. (IDK was started by diversity workers to explore the vast space with regard to racism that we characterize as "I Don't Know.")

Telling the story in written form has been possible only because people who know and care have listened us into writing, again and again. Foremost, in their stalwart support, are two people without whom we would not have gotten our story this far: Margot Silk Forrest, an award-winning writer in her own right, who has edited several versions of this manuscript and listened us into more and more of it, tirelessly, and with grace and appreciation for who we are and what we're trying to do; and Art Kleiner, a man of many incarnations, currently the editor of s*trategy+business*, who has believed in this story every step of the way and urged us to go ahead with it, even though it's not as uplifting, happy or generative as we believe it should be before we put it out.

We feel the deepest gratitude to: Brenda Joyner, Diane Woods, Barbara Harris and Diane Rizzetto for seeing our story as one of hope and triumph; Adam Kahane for helping us think into the next version of the story and for his wonderful foreword; Jay Davidson for painstaking grammar and punctuation review, volunteered in the last hours after we could do no more; Rita Sandhu, Rhoberta Hirtir, Sid Reel, Mark Albion and Bob Sadler for helping us think about the talks, workshops, collaborations, consulting and much needed income stream to grow out of this book; Ken Homer for his deep and heartfelt questions that can inspire next steps for readers and all of us with regard to ending racism; Diane Woods, for holding a vast field of possibility for all of us in this work and for always bringing food; and Laurie Mittelstadt for being there time and again when the Mack Trucks hit and for bringing food.

Thank you, too, dear readers, for reading and responding to our call. We look forward to responding to yours. That's what progress on "things racial" is all about. You can reach us by email at thingsracial@gmail.com and through our website, www.thingsracial.com .

FOR MORE INFORMATION

To learn more about Stacy and Barb's work and lives, download free resources, schedule a talk with Stacy about doing a workshop with her and Diane Woods, or ask a question, visit:

www.thingsracial.com

Made in the USA
Charleston, SC
19 July 2011